CONSTELLATION "HEROES"

Tracing David Bowie's Berlin Album Song By Song

Hans Meertens

SONICBOND

sonicbondpublishing.com

Sonicbond Publishing Limited
www.sonicbondpublishing.co.uk
Email: info@sonicbondpublishing.co.uk

First Published in the United Kingdom 2026
First Published in the United States 2026

British Library Cataloguing in Publication Data:
A Catalogue record for this book is available from the British Library

ISBN 978-1-78952-498-7

Typeset in ITC Garamond Std & ITC Avant Garde Gothic
Printed and bound in England

Graphic design and typesetting: Full Moon Media

Follow us on social media:
Twitter: https://twitter.com/SonicbondP
Instagram: www.instagram.com/sonicbondpublishing_/
Facebook: www.facebook.com/SonicbondPublishing/

Linktree QR code:

Acknowledgements

This book began with the wish to trace, illuminate and reflect, and to contribute fresh and meaningful perspectives to the interpretation of *"Heroes"* within the historiography of David Bowie, alongside the many volumes already written about him. The most insightful of these, to my mind, are listed in the selected bibliography.

I am also indebted to the photographers whose images are included in this book, and grateful to Magnolia Pictures for their assistance in licensing one of them. My special gratitude goes to Ilan Deutsch for his generous permission to include a photograph from the Jean-Claude Deutsch archive, and to Arthur D'Amario III and Roger Woolman. Further thanks go to Kevin Armstrong, Eduard Meyer, Joost Jan Meertens, Paul Roeters and Stephen Lambe, whose belief in the project led to its realisation through Sonicbond Publishing.

This book is dedicated to my parents,
who never died but just went to sleep one day.

I like complications.
I like things that seem to be endless puzzles.
I like thickly textured things.
David Bowie, press conference for the European *Outside Tour*, 1995

Berlin is a skeleton which aches in the cold: it is my own skeleton aching.
Christopher Isherwood, *Goodbye To Berlin*, 1939

Art doesn't have a purpose. It's a free spot in society where you can do anything.
Chris Burden, *Coast*, 1974

These fragments I have shored against my ruins.
T. S. Eliot, *The Waste Land*, 1922

CONSTELLATION "HEROES"

Contents

Introduction

This is not the life story of David Bowie. It is the story of *"Heroes"*. Instead of tracing his career in full, it speaks to readers already immersed in his work, especially those drawn to the Berlin years and the albums that emerged from them. It focuses on a constellation of songs, locations and circumstances: the period from 1976 to 1979, when *"Heroes"* was forged amid the city's fractured atmosphere.

That Berlin myth has been widely retold in biographies, interviews, blogs and podcasts. Tony Visconti and Carlos Alomar have frequently shared their memories, and Bowie himself revisited that chapter often, each time through a different lens. While much of the surrounding history may be familiar to dedicated Bowie fans, this book returns to that story with closer attention to undercurrents, hidden continuities and lyric readings that offer new angles. Rather than centring on studio technique or chord structures, this approach follows an interpretive journey through image, association and mood. It seeks to uncover how the motifs unfold, the tangled mesh of cultural signals they carry, and why this record continues to reverberate like a monument caught in motion.

Bowie remains an artist who invites interpretation. While countless books survey his life and career, few pause long enough over a single album. A sustained study allows for greater richness and precision. As with *Low*, the lyrics on *"Heroes"* are routinely described as short, fragmentary and disjointed. That may be fair, yet it is precisely why they reward patient reading. This book examines how those jagged pieces hold meaning, weaving historical forces, personal ruptures and artistic references into a cross-cultural, expressionist collage.

Like many in my generation, I discovered Bowie only after his great 1970s albums had already been released, catching him live across the years. Exploring his back catalogue as a teenager was one of the most exhilarating, revelatory and enduring musical experiences of my life. Before I owned the records, I relied on copied cassette tapes. I would cycle to the local record store, pull out the inner sleeves and try to decipher lyrics I could only half make out. No other artist has sparked the same depth of fascination, admiration, or lasting impact. For countless fans, myself included, Bowie was a portal: to other voices, other artists, other worlds. He didn't just create culture, he connected it across music, art, literature and film. Without him, I might never have gone to art school.

Choosing a single Bowie album as the main subject of this book was no easy task. With few exceptions, his entire body of work earns its place among the all time greats: *Hunky Dory*, *Ziggy Stardust*, *Aladdin Sane*, *Station To Station*, *Low*, *Scary Monsters*, *Let's Dance*, *Blackstar*. Each stands as a landmark in its own right. Over the four decades I have spent living with these records, *"Heroes"* may be the one that has grown the most: in ambiguity, in gravity, in scope. What tugged at it, perhaps, was something more elusive.

The Berlin of *"Heroes"* felt charged: a capitalist island adrift in a communist sea. Cold War unease and spies, post-war shadows, the Wall looming like an open wound, history still pulsing beneath the concrete. The cover mirrored that strain: black-and-white, angular, the *Roquairol* pose taut with Schiele tension. It looked like a still from a lost Weimar-era film. Songs circle around Florian Schneider, body art, collapse. A sudden shift eastward on a more global scale: a different kind of minimalism, a different kind of mystery. The final track steps beyond the known world altogether: a windswept, cinematic desert, the death of a heroine, another myth, another geography, another code.

Guitars screech. Vocals waver between detachment and devotion. Nothing settles. This is not solid ground. The moment you try to pin it down, the album fractures and reforms. The fascination that fuelled this book lies exactly where the record itself dwells: between East and West, between selves, between worlds. Everything gestures towards something – Berlin, Japan, Arabia, defiance, art, cabaret, dreams, alcohol – but nothing ever resolves. Meaning is always implied, never fixed. Listening to *"Heroes"* is like walking through a city you've known for years, only to find yourself lost in it again. The signs are familiar, but the streets keep bending.

The lyrics unfold in fragments: needling, at times mordant and always bristling with intent. They flare and fade like sparks from a live wire, conjuring images that linger even as they dissolve. Tonal echoes, veiled allusions and sidelong nods drift through Bowie's earlier songs into the ghosted, liminal space where these new ones took shape. Bowie's voice is magnificently attuned to this terrain: committed, histrionic, fervent. From sonorous baritone to full-throated cries and piercing falsetto, it stretches and splinters, never holding back, always reaching for the emotional edge.

"Heroes" is the crack in the wall, the swell of freedom, the manic heartbeat of a man reinventing himself in a city poised on the fault line. A lean figure prowls through a desolate border zone: concrete slick with neon, flashes splitting the gloom, the air pierced by bursts of ungovernable sound, or brushed by spectral shapes that vanish as you turn.

Watch That Man

In January 1947, Berlin was a shattered city in a divided land. The ruins of war were everywhere: burnt-out buildings, collapsed bridges, whole districts reduced to rubble. Daily life unfolded among wreckage, black markets and makeshift shelters. The city was carved into four sectors: American, British, French and Soviet. Tensions between the former allies were steadily rising. The Cold War had yet to be named, but it was already being felt in growing restrictions, arrests and mutual suspicion.

Food was scarce, coal rationed and electricity unreliable. Women and children survived through barter and smuggling. Yet amid the destruction, signs of renewal began to appear. Schools reopened in stages, newspapers returned and the first stirrings of culture resurfaced. Many Nazis had gone underground or quietly resumed official roles. Denazification was patchy. Some war criminals were in custody, others were back behind desks. The mood was tense, raw and weary. But Berlin endured. In the shadow of the past, a new age was hesitantly beginning.

Across the Channel, David Robert Jones was born on 8 January 1947 in Brixton, South London, and raised in the suburban sprawl of Bromley. The city around him was still pocked with bomb damage, scarred by the Blitz and the later V-1 and V-2 attacks. Londoners were queuing in the cold for bread, meat and coal. His father, Haywood Stenton 'John' Jones, worked as a promotions officer at the children's charity Barnardo's. Together with his wife, Margaret Mary 'Peggy' Jones, he kept a modest lower-middle-class household. David had two half-sisters, Annette and Myra, from his parents' earlier relationships, but neither lived with the family nor played a meaningful role in his upbringing. More formative was the presence of a third half-sibling: through Peggy, there was Terence – known as 'Terry' – ten years his senior, who lived with the family until 1955 and whose outlook and interests left a strong early mark.

A sharp-minded, imaginative boy with a fascination for music and myth, young Davie showed early signs of wanting to become more than just another kid in a suit. As a teenager, he played saxophone and sang in a series of short-lived R&B bands, including The Konrads, The King Bees, The Manish Boys and The Lower Third. By the mid-1960s, he had dropped the name Davie Jones, adopted the name David Bowie and embarked on a solo career.

In the years that followed, he released a string of singles and a debut album shaped by Anthony Newley's influence before finding his first brush with fame in 1969. 'Space Oddity', released just ahead of the Apollo 11 moon landing, launched him into the charts with uncanny timing. The song featured on his second album, a blend of folk rock and layered lyricism that merged acoustic textures with a growing taste for amplified sound. But the success was fragile. *The Man Who Sold The World* veered into heavier terrain, pairing Nietzschean imagery with proto-metal guitars, while *Hunky Dory* offered elegance, introspection and melodic brilliance. Both albums were critically admired but modest in sales.

Everything changed with *The Rise And Fall Of Ziggy Stardust And The Spiders From Mars*. The Ziggy persona, an androgynous alien rock star who burned bright and fast, blurred the line between theatre and reality, song and identity. Bowie's mix of camp, craft and conviction created a new kind of pop hero, one that embodied the fantasies and anxieties of a generation. Britain in 1972, shaped by post-war drift, economic gloom and the fading promises of the 1960s, was grey and confused, but aching for change. Ziggy was a revolution: thrilling for teenagers, unsettling for parents and impossible to ignore.

He took the character to America, observed its chaos and glamour, and turned the experience into *Aladdin Sane*: a splintered road trip through decadence and urban decay, wired on amphetamine flash. His shows grew larger, more intense, the persona harder to shake. At the height of Ziggy-mania, he abruptly killed off the character onstage, half liberation, half collapse. By then, he had become one of the biggest music stars in Britain, with *Aladdin Sane* debuting at number one and selling over 100,000 copies in its first week. In the US, it cracked the *Billboard* top 20, giving Bowie his first real foothold across the Atlantic.

Along the way, he co-produced Lou Reed's *Transformer*, helped Mott The Hoople revive their fortunes with 'All The Young Dudes' and mixed Iggy And The Stooges' *Raw Power*. He also produced Lulu's hit cover of 'The Man Who Sold The World' during breaks from work on *Pin Ups*, his 1960s tribute album. Even that detour shot straight to number one in the UK, proof of just how high Bowie was flying. His next step, *Diamond Dogs*, painted a grotesque dystopia haunted by Orwell and Burgess, teetering on the edge of cabaret and collapse. The album came on like Ziggy's hangover sealed inside a totalitarian hallucination, set in the crumbling, diseased sprawl of Hunger City. Staged like a piece of mutant Broadway, the *Diamond Dogs Tour* in 1974 featured a $250,000 backdrop inspired by *The Cabinet Of Dr. Caligari*, and saw Bowie move on from the flamboyance of Ziggy and Aladdin Sane. Still theatrical, he appeared as Halloween Jack in a sharp pale blue two-piece suit with suspenders and a patterned knit: a transitional aesthetic, midway between glam's visual excess and a colder, more narcotised presence beginning to stir beneath the surface.

During a break in the tour, Bowie began recording *Young Americans*, driven by a growing pull towards Philly soul and crisp, funky musicianship. When the tour resumed, the lavish Hunger City set was gone. Bowie had discovered that the financial structure set up by his manager, Tony Defries of MainMan, had effectively made him a thief of his own earnings. Business tensions were mounting, and he completed the remaining shows under stripped-down conditions as the *Soul Tour*.

In *Cracked Actor*, the BBC documentary filmed during this phase, Bowie appears emaciated, anxious and clearly strung out on cocaine. His speech is articulate but often erratic, veering between sharp insight and moments of disconnection. In one scene, he cuts up strips of handwritten lyrics, demonstrating the cut-up method he had adopted from William S. Burroughs, whom he had met in 1973. Burroughs' description of semen in *Naked Lunch* as 'the thin white rope' may well have fed into the name of Bowie's next stage character, whose silhouette was already forming in the stylised hustler suits he began wearing in early 1975.

In March of that year, he released *Young Americans*, which marked his commercial breakthrough in the US. The album reached the top ten on the *Billboard* chart, with 'Fame' becoming his first number one single. The funk-infused track, co-written by Bowie, John Lennon and Carlos Alomar and driven by Alomar's snapping guitar line, was a bitter reflection on his recently severed ties with Defries and the MainMan company. Financial strain lingered, as MainMan had burned through money with reckless abandon, leaving Bowie to foot the bill. The pressure of drawn-out disputes weighed heavily, and his cocaine use spiralled. In interviews, he came across as increasingly paranoid, agitated and incoherent. His obsessions would take ever stranger turns, veering into occultism, UFOs, conspiracy theories, the Kabbalah and a growing fascination with Nazi mysticism.

When Nicolas Roeg saw Bowie's fragile presence in *Cracked Actor*, he knew immediately that this was his Thomas Jerome Newton for the film version of Walter Tevis' 1963 novel *The Man Who Fell To Earth,* centred on a stranded alien among humans. Bowie was ready to embody a being on the brink: cinema was a natural extension of his ongoing shape-shifting, and Newton offered the most radical, inward project of his career. He moved from New York to LA in the spring, and filming for *The Man Who Fell To Earth* took place that summer in the stark heat of New Mexico. Bowie was in a precarious state of mind. Reflecting on that period, he told *Movieline* in 1992:

> I actually was feeling as alienated as that character was. It was a pretty natural performance ... a good exhibition of somebody literally falling apart in front of you. I was totally insecure with about ten grams a day in me. I was stoned out of my mind from beginning to end.

Pale, untethered and barely eating, he was gently urged to put on some weight, reportedly coaxed with bowls of ice cream, and somehow managed to carry the shoot with discipline, earning quiet respect from the crew for his focus and professionalism. Most of his downtime was spent reading in his trailer or in a modest ranch-style home arranged by his personal assistant, Corinne 'Coco' Schwab. He had brought hundreds of books with him, delving deeper into the occult philosophies of Aleister Crowley, Edward Waite and Dion Fortune, while scanning the desert night skies for signs of extraterrestrial life. He also worked on a collection of short stories, loosely anchored in autobiography but drifting far into fiction, laced with spectral symbolism and magical logic. The working title: *The Return Of The Thin White Duke.*

The Babylon Cut

Bowie had befriended Deep Purple bassist Glenn Hughes in 1974, when the *Diamond Dogs Tour* reached LA. The two bonded quickly, drawn together by music and mutual excess, and were inseparable that summer. Almost a year later, in the lead-up to the filming of *The Man Who Fell To Earth*, Bowie stayed at Hughes' place in Beverly Hills. 'I was in Germany, but he came anyway, by train, alone ... which was incredible for one of the world's biggest stars. I arrived home five days later', Hughes told *Louder Sound* in 2016. 'He was seeing things in the sky and drawing them on my windows in crayon.'

After a brief stint living with Hughes, Bowie moved into a rented house on Doheny Drive, flanked in the garden by two white sphinxes. That marked the beginning of his most hallucinatory period in LA. One night, Hughes and Elton John drummer Nigel Olsson found themselves at the property, where a sleepless, skeletal Bowie became convinced the devil was lurking in his swimming pool. He insisted Hughes wade in, fully clothed, to search for it. 'He was out of his mind, we both were, and I say that out of love. He was wafer-thin. I scarcely remember seeing him sleep, but when he did so, it was for days at a time', Hughes remembered.

The madness only deepened. Consumed by the decadent excesses of Hollywood, Bowie's time in LA gave rise to a catalogue of grimly comic myths: a diet of nothing but red peppers, milk and cocaine; jars of bodily fluids stored in the fridge to keep witches from stealing his soul; a mystic-led exorcism on his pool; black candles burning, bodies glimpsed falling past the window, and endless days watching Fritz Lang films and Nazi propaganda behind drawn curtains. 'By the end of the week, my whole life would be transformed into this bizarre, nihilistic fantasy world of oncoming doom, mythological characters and imminent totalitarianism. Quite the worst', Bowie told *Musician* in 1983. 'Cocaine is the devil's drug', Hughes is quoted as saying in *David Bowie: The Oral History*. 'There was a moment when we were getting high, and David started to bleed from his eye, actually bleeding.' Whether exaggerated or not, such stories all point to the same truth: Bowie was unravelling. The Thin White Duke persona, soon to emerge, would not be a mere theatrical creation but a reflection of his reality.

His marriage to Angela 'Angie' Barnett was marked by growing psychological distance and increasing physical separation. She had found the house on Doheny Drive, but they spent little time there together. Their open arrangement meant an ongoing stream of other partners on both sides, while their own time together dwindled. At the same time, Bowie's deepening reliance on Coco became a steady source of tension. The end of their marriage was only a matter of time.

It was in this darkened state of personal, physical and psychological deterioration that Bowie wrapped filming for *The Man Who Fell To Earth* and began channelling himself more fully into the film's soundtrack and his own next album. Coco secured him a quiet haven on Stone Canyon Road in Bel

Air, still within reach of Hollywood's creative pulse. Just over five miles away, Cherokee Studios sat at the heart of the city's burgeoning recording scene.

Having already produced four of his albums, including *David Live,* Bowie initially wanted long-time friend and collaborator Tony Visconti to helm what would become his tenth studio record, which he had only just begun to envision alongside the soundtrack work. With Visconti unavailable, he turned to 'Fame' producer Harry Maslin to co-produce the new material. For the core band, he brought in *Young Americans* guitarist Carlos Alomar, drummer Dennis Davis, who had played on the late additions 'Across The Universe' and 'Fame', and bassist George Murray, who had toured with George McCrae and performed in Broadway productions. The three would become known as the DAM trio: a tight, versatile rhythm section grounded in soul, jazz and funk. Their precision and feel would help define Bowie's sound both live and in the studio for the next five years. The group was completed by guitarist Earl Slick from the *Diamond Dogs Tour* and *Young Americans*, and pianist Roy Bittan of Bruce Springsteen's E Street Band.

In a nocturnal fever of coke and occult delirium, with just a couple of songs and only the barest sketches beyond that, the recording rites spiralled into an ecstatic trance of improvised intensity and cryptic imagery. The result was a propulsive masterpiece. *Station To Station* finally summoned the Thin White Duke, a presence both austere and possessed, singing of spiritual despair, the Stations of the Cross, the pursuit of connection and love, and a girl-eating TV. It was a brilliant glimpse into the mind of a man who had spent months portraying an alien on screen, at a time when no one remembered if he had ever been anything else. The record carries religious, mystical and psychological overtones all at once, set against a fusion of soul, rock, funk and the first tentative steps into colder European waters.

'I'm doing the soundtrack for *The Man Who Fell To Earth* with a friend of mine, Paul Buckmaster', Bowie said during a November taping of *Soul Train*, where he drunkenly mimed along to 'Fame' and premiered his new single, 'Golden Years'. When he accepted the role, the plan had been for RCA to back the production, with Bowie's score doubling as a promotional tool for the film. It was a prospect he welcomed, broadening his scope as a composer. For the project, he turned to Buckmaster, the classically trained arranger whose orchestral work had left a distinct mark on 'Space Oddity', which had recently re-entered the UK charts, climbing to number one. With *Station To Station* nearing completion, Bowie and Buckmaster began work on a modest TEAC four-track recorder at Bowie's Bel Air home before moving to Cherokee Studios, where they were joined by the DAM trio and J Peter Robinson on Fender Rhodes and synthesiser.

While those sessions resulted in a couple of medium-tempo instrumentals built around riffs and funk-inflected grooves, Bowie and Buckmaster concentrated on slower, more atmospheric pieces, including a song Bowie wrote, performed and sang, titled 'Wheels', and an early version of what would later evolve into the *Low* track 'Subterraneans'. With Bowie's guitar and Buckmaster's cello set against electronic textures, including ARP Odyssey, Solina and ring-modulated piano, the compositions echoed faint traces of Kraftwerk's recently released *Radio-Activity*. Fuelled by his constant drive for change and reinvention, Bowie had already absorbed Kraftwerk and was gravitating towards a broader range of experimental German bands – Cluster, Faust, Neu!, Popol Vuh, Tangerine Dream and CAN – whose work spanned ambient collages, motorik grooves, feedback guitar and tape-based improvisation, while Kraftwerk made the leap to fully electronic precision.

By the end of December, the sessions had yielded only five or six working tracks. 'I considered the music to be demo-ish and not final, although we were supposed to be making it final. All we produced was something substandard, and Nic Roeg turned it down on those grounds ...' Buckmaster told *Mojo* in 2007. Bowie withdrew all of his contributions after being told he would need to submit his compositions alongside tracks by other artists. He told *NME* in 1980:

> It turned out for the better, and, of course, it did prompt me in another area – to consider my own instrumental capabilities, which I hadn't really done very seriously before. The area was one that was suddenly exciting me, one that I never really considered would. And that's when I got the first inklings of trying to work with Eno at some point.

Although the novel, soon to be reissued to coincide with the film, already carried 'Music By Bowie' on its back cover, John Phillips, former leader of 1960s hitmakers The Mamas & The Papas, was subsequently brought in to assemble the soundtrack in London. Bowie would later send an early copy of *Low* to Roeg with a note: 'This is what I wanted to do for the soundtrack.' Roeg agreed it would have been a wonderful score.

Bowie's lost soundtrack now stands as a ghostly bridge between the Hollywood Abaddon Opus he had crafted and the records that would follow, transforming his sound, his state of mind and the course of his life. With a number one hit in the country he had long wanted to conquer, a starring role in a big-screen sci-fi fantasy about to premiere and a new album ready for release, Bowie seemed to have made it in America. But as he recalled in a 1983 interview with *Musician*, he was already yearning to leave:

> The overriding need for me was to develop more of a European influence, having immersed myself so thoroughly in American culture. As I was personally going through a very bad time, I thought I had to get back to Europe.

But first, the Duke would step into the spotlight. Travelling with him: a heroin-addicted Detroit proto-punk, just as desperate to escape the Hollywood snakepit.

White Light Transit

Under a hard wash of white light, the Thin White Duke materialised: slicked-back hair, black waistcoat, white shirt, a pack of Gitanes tucked neatly into one pocket. The stage was flooded in icy brilliance, lit from above by neon strips and searing Klieg lights that bleached it into stark monochrome. The effect was theatrical in its severity: an expressionist glare that sharpened both the music's attack and Bowie's own silhouette as a French matinee Dracula of cabaret control. Detached and mesmerising, he radiated focus without warmth, like a flicker sealed inside frosted glass. The construct was born of the psychic wreckage of Thomas Jerome Newton, whose descent mirrored Bowie's own. In 1978, Bowie described the Duke in *Crawdaddy* as 'a very Aryan, fascist type; a would-be romantic with absolutely no emotion at all but who spouted a lot of neoromance.'

Two weeks after turning 29, Bowie released *Station To Station*, his highest-charting US album, which peaked at number three and also reached the top ten in Australia, the Netherlands, France, New Zealand, Norway and the UK. The sessions that produced it had already slipped into a fug, and would remain that way. 'I can't even remember the studio', Bowie told VH1 in 1997. 'I know it was in LA 'cause I've read it was in LA.' He took it on the road as the *Isolar Tour*, now more widely remembered as the *White Light* or *Station To Station Tour*. From February to May, it travelled through Canada, the US and Europe, earning praise from both audiences and critics. The album's monolithic drive found its match on stage, where the music's austere grandeur was mirrored in a stylised production shaped by the shadows and severity of Lang and Pabst. Behind the scenes, a curious observer followed closely, taking in the stagecraft and rigour, then joining the parties after dark. His name was Jim Osterberg, known to the world as Iggy Pop.

Iggy had made chaos and history with The Stooges before the band disintegrated in 1974, undone by poor sales and the wreckage of heroin-fuelled self-destruction. Bowie had been an early supporter, befriending Iggy back in 1971, and had mixed their album *Raw Power*, the band's final studio album of that era. After the collapse, Iggy drifted between New York and LA, unmoored, gaunt and chemically undone. Friends found him incoherent, volatile, vanishing before their eyes. By 1975, his decline had become such a public nuisance that the LAPD gave him a choice: jail or rehab. He chose the Neuropsychiatric Institute at UCLA. Bowie was one of the few who visited, offering support and, in a murky gesture of loyalty, bringing a sizeable amount of drugs. After his release, Bowie arranged a demo session in LA to launch Iggy's solo career, but it quickly fell apart. He was still erratic, in no state to work.

Nearly a year later, Iggy was still adrift, living as chaotically as Bowie but without his discipline and resources. After being caught shoplifting apples and cheese in Beverly Hills, their mutual dealer bailed him out and told him that Bowie wanted to reconnect and work together again, and Iggy got in touch. The chemistry was still intact. Bowie invited him to join the touring entourage as a companion, a friend, maybe even to tinker with new ideas. Iggy took four days to decide. With no real way out of the wreckage, he agreed. The ride would offer no shortage of defining and disorienting moments.

In Rochester, a post-show party in Bowie's hotel suite ended in a drug bust. At 2.25 am, narcotics officers charged Bowie, his bodyguard, Iggy and a young Rochester woman with possession of eight ounces of marijuana. They spent several hours in jail before Bowie posted bond for the group. The case was effectively dropped when a Grand Jury declined to indict. Speaking to *Playboy* later that year, Bowie shrugged: 'Bloody potheads. What a dreadful irony – me popped for grass. The stuff sickens me.'

During the European leg of the tour, Bowie drew criticism for a series of controversial political remarks. In an interview with *Rolling Stone*, conducted during the occult-infused madness of the previous summer and published that February, he had spoken of his fascination with power and dictatorship: 'I think I might have been a bloody good Hitler. I'd be an excellent dictator. Very eccentric and quite mad.' He described himself as 'certainly right-wing enough' to become either Prime Minister of Britain or President of the United States.

While the controversy simmered, the tour moved deeper into Europe. In Berlin, Bowie and Iggy crossed at Checkpoint Charlie and drove through East Berlin in Bowie's rickety limousine, absorbing the heavy stillness of the divided city. With a week before the next concert in Helsinki, they made a side trip by train to Moscow via Warsaw. At the Polish-Soviet border, they were detained by the KGB and strip-searched. Among Bowie's belongings were books on Goebbels and Speer, which he described as research for a planned film about Hitler's propaganda minister. In Moscow, they visited Red Square and the GUM department store, ate caviar at the Metropol, then left the city by train seven hours after arrival. At his next stop in Helsinki, the newspaper headline the following day read: 'Bowie Lost in Russia!' From there, he travelled on to Sweden. At a press meeting after the Stockholm concert, Bowie was confronted by a journalist about the *Rolling Stone* remarks. Asked whether he still believed that Britain needed a fascist leader, he replied, 'Oh yes, not a Nazi leader, a fascist leader', adding that people 'won't know what they really want until they are ruled.' The remarks were published the next day and caused immediate controversy in the British press.

A week later, on 2 May, Bowie arrived at Victoria Station in London and was photographed with his arm raised in a gesture that could be construed as a Nazi salute. *NME* published the image under the headline 'HEIL AND FAREWELL', offering no clarification or supporting context. 'It upsets me. Strong, I may be. Arrogant, I may be. Sinister, I'm not', he told the *Daily Express* three days after the incident. Film footage suggests he had merely been waving to the crowd, a version he consistently maintained in subsequent statements and which was later corroborated by Gary Numan and photographer Philippe Auliac, both present that day. 'I just waved. Believe me. On the life of my child, I waved. And the bastard caught me. In mid-wave, man. And, God, did that photo get some coverage ...' Bowie would tell *Melody Maker* in 1977.

But the damage had been done. The combination of the pose and his recent comments cemented the perception of an artist aligning himself with authoritarian posturing, amplified by the Aryan froideur of the Thin White Duke and earlier allusions to Nietzschean visions of the future. It is hard to miss how his cocaine-fuelled immersion in Nazi occult mythologies, from Arthurian Grail quests to the imagined power of the Spear of Destiny, fed into his lapses at a time when his public statements were already under scrutiny.

The fallout would echo in September 1976, when *Playboy* published an interview conducted before the Victoria Station incident, in which Bowie again made provocative comments. One of them: 'I believe very strongly in fascism.' He praised the efficiency of fascist regimes in contrast with liberalism's indecision, and likened Hitler's stagecraft to that of Mick Jagger, before dismissing such remarks as 'inflammatory' in the same conversation. In retrospect, Bowie had been drawn to the theatrical force of propaganda for its aesthetics and perceived potency, rather than any political ideology. 'What I said was Britain was ready for another Hitler, which is quite a different thing from saying it needs another Hitler. I'm closer to communism than fascism – that at least has some saving graces', he told *Record Mirror* in 1977. In *Popster* the same year, he stated: 'All the statements I've made are 'theatrical warnings'. I am completely nonpartisan.'

Whether driven by shock tactics, cocaine delusion, or obsessive intellectual curiosity, the controversies in 1976 proved difficult to shake off and led to speculation over whether Bowie should also be seen as racist. His face appeared on 'Rock Against Racism' leaflets, and the backlash only intensified the dangerous allure of the Thin White Duke myth. In later interviews, he repeatedly distanced himself from the remarks, insisting they did not reflect his personal convictions. In 1993, he told *Arena* that he had equated fascism with communism, specifically Stalinism, adding: 'It's hard to see that you could get involved with all that and not see the implications of what you were getting into.' He consistently blamed his erratic behaviour and his dalliances with fascist rhetoric and occultism on drug-induced paranoia and depression. 'I was out of my mind, totally, completely crazed. Really. But the main thing I was functioning on was – as far as that whole thing about Hitler and rightism was concerned – it was mythology', he told *NME* in 1980:

> This whole racist thing, which came up quite inevitably and rightly. But – and I know this sounds terribly naive – but none of that had actually occurred to me, inasmuch as I'd been working, and still do work, with black musicians for the past six or seven years. And we'd all talk about it together

> – about the Arthurian period, about the magical side of the whole Nazi campaign, and about the mythology involved. All that stuff was flying around, buzzing around the skies.

In 1993, he addressed the issue in *NME* again: 'The idea that it was about putting Jews in concentration camps and the complete oppression of different races completely evaded my extraordinary fucked-up nature at that particular time.' During his later career, Bowie repeatedly and publicly challenged racism. Most notably, he confronted MTV in 1983 over its exclusion of Black artists, supported anti-racist causes, and took that fight into several songs. Although he regarded the *Station To Station Tour* as one of his most theatrically successful, by the end of the run, he exorcised its ghostly aristocrat altogether. 'The Thin White Duke was a very nasty character indeed', he said in *Record Mirror* in 1977.

Other encounters on the tour would plant more fertile seeds. In February, backstage at the Inglewood Forum in LA, Bowie was visited by Christopher Isherwood. The British expatriate, by then in his early 70s, responded to Bowie's curiosity with memories of Weimar Berlin, where he had lived during the final years of the republic. Isherwood's 1935 novel *Mr Norris Changes Trains* later appeared in Bowie's published list of his 100 favourite books, while *Goodbye To Berlin* from 1939 had also reached him through its 1972 film adaptation, *Cabaret*. Both works portrayed the German capital as a feverish carnival of sex, squalor and suspense, teetering on the edge of catastrophe. Although Isherwood downplayed their accuracy and reminded Bowie he was, above all, a fiction writer, hearing the stories first-hand, from the man himself, gave them renewed urgency.

During the tour's stop at Wembley's Empire Pool, Bowie reconnected with Brian Eno, the pioneering sound experimentalist and former Roxy Music keyboardist. They had first crossed paths in 1972, when Roxy Music briefly opened for Ziggy Stardust, and had followed each other's work ever since. Bowie had been playing *Discreet Music* obsessively during the American leg and now told Eno how much it had meant to him. In *Uncut* in 1999, Eno recalled thinking: 'God, he must be smart!' That night, they talked deep into the early hours, drawn together by shared obsessions and a kindred taste for aural invention and post-pop strategies. By the end of the evening, plans to collaborate were already forming.

Other sonic adventurers would cross his path, too. After meeting Ralf Hütter and Florian Schneider of Kraftwerk during the German leg of the tour in Düsseldorf, Bowie invited them to the aftershow party following his penultimate concert in Paris. The next night, Bowie celebrated the tour's end at L'Alcazar with Romy Haag, the flamboyant cabaret star he had first encountered in Berlin and whose milieu would later play a part in drawing him back to the city. By then, his thoughts were already turning towards a return to Europe: a way to escape the Hollywood frenzy, recharge his music with new European inspiration and immerse himself in a different environment. There was also the burden of a crippling tax bill if he stayed in America or went back to England. Angie had proposed Switzerland as a tax haven and had already set about finding housing.

When the tour wrapped on 18 May, Bowie, Iggy and Coco planned to remain in Paris, but the hotel was under siege from fans at all hours. As a retreat, they headed to Château d'Hérouville, the faded 18th-century manor and studio just outside the city where Bowie had recorded *Pin Ups* in 1973. Known as the Honky Château, the residential studio offered them a few days of quiet, away from the commotion. Bowie met studio manager Laurent Thibault, played him records and booked the Château for June and July to start recording Iggy's debut solo album. RCA would cover the costs, a relief for Bowie at a time when his split with MainMan had choked off his royalties. After a few days, he left with his five-year-old son Zowie and his nanny to join Angie in Switzerland, where she had arranged to rent a chalet in Blonay near Montreux. There, he began sketching new musical ideas on a small cassette machine, soon joined by Iggy as they roughed out the first songs for *The Idiot*. Two of the finest albums of their careers were already in the making.

The Idiot Lab

The recording of *The Idiot* began in June 1976, with Bowie laying down skeletal tracks on his Baldwin electric piano at the Château. What had started as an intimate two-man operation quickly grew into a more ambitious venture. Bowie requested a drummer, and engineer Thibault, now doubling on bass, brought in Michel Santangeli, a session player who assumed he was there for demos. He left after two days, unaware that his first takes would end up on the final album.

From the start, the sound veered sharply away from anything Iggy had recorded before. Gone were the loose guitars and ragged propulsion of The Stooges. In their place: treated drums, fragmented guitar figures and textures borrowed more from European electronics than American rock. Bowie wasn't just producing, but he was building a new vocabulary. 'Poor Jim, in a way, became a guinea pig for what I wanted to do with sound', Bowie said in the 1989 *Sound+Vision* liner notes. 'I didn't have the material at the time, and I didn't feel like writing at all. I felt much more like lying back and getting behind someone else's work, so that album was opportune, creatively.'

Working from Bowie's sonic palette of guitar, synthesisers, saxophone and backing vocals, Iggy began improvising lyrics at the microphone, drawing on scenes from the road and flashes of private obsession. Bowie was fascinated by his instinctive wordplay: 'I thought he was the funniest, darkest lyricist of the time', he said in *Seconds* in 1995. The sessions were a creative burst: books and handwritten lyrics on the floor, tape reels running, meals skipped, the two of them throwing ideas at each other with instinctive speed. 'I think I functioned as an outlet for his overflow. Because there are things he did with me that he couldn't do as David Bowie, because it would have slowed him down or might have been a wrong move', Iggy told *Uncut* in 2006. 'And then he was also able to use me to practice ... He made an Iggy album first, but watched the engineers there in the studio, learned how they worked, thought about it, had a chance to get to know the desk, and had daydreams about his own record while he worked on mine.'

By late July, Davis and Murray arrived for Bowie's next album, and were credited for additional rhythmic framework on *The Idiot*. One afternoon, another visitor arrived: Kuelan Nguyen, the Vietnamese partner of French actor and singer Jacques Higelin, who had been invited to the Château by its owner. Despite the language barrier and Nguyen's relationship, she and Iggy began a brief affair that directly inspired one of the album's standout tracks.

When the Château became unavailable in August, sessions moved to Musicland Studios in Munich, where they worked through the night beneath the Sheraton hotel, with Phil Palmer, nephew of Ray Davies, adding guitar parts. Additional vocals were also recorded at Musicland, often veering into overmodulated distortion that etched a piercing edge into Iggy's signature tone. The album was completed at Hansa Tonstudio 1 in Berlin, where Visconti salvaged the mix, grappling with saturated tracks and smoothing their murky edges in post-production. 'When I came to mix the tracks, I found they were a mess; it was because of a cry for help that I was back in Berlin', he later wrote in his autobiography, *Bowie, Bolan And The Brooklyn Boy*. It was the trio's first encounter with the Hansa complex: a calm, westward-facing studio in Halensee's quiet residential streets, a measured prelude to the more disquieting atmosphere of Tonstudio 2 by the Wall.

The Idiot would reach number 72 on the *Billboard* chart in 1977 and crack the UK top 40, a first for Iggy. For Bowie, the album marked a private breakthrough: a move beyond American rock's established tropes, towards something austere, starker and more European in tone. Though guitars still sliced through the mix, the album absorbed the avant-garde spirit of Kraftwerk, Neu!, CAN and Faust. Rhythms were rigid, textures scorched and the synthesisers sounded less like melody than machine.

Among its eight tracks are 'Sister Midnight', born from a tour rehearsal jam, retaining Bowie's skeletal vocal phrasing and Alomar's circular funk riff, twisted by Iggy's overtly Oedipal lyrics. 'Nightclubbing', built around a preset Roland rhythm box, evokes the ghostlike decadence of Bowie and Iggy's nocturnal drift. Inspired by Iggy's dissonant romance with Nguyen, 'China Girl' began as a quiet sketch and developed into an intensifying fever whose pop potential surfaced only later. The *Metropolis* machinery of 'Mass Production' closes the album with metallic churn and dissonant grind, driven by Bowie's abrasive synths, spiralling into industrial dread.

Its influence proved long and far-reaching. Joy Division, Bauhaus, Gary Numan, The Human League, Killing Joke, The Sisters Of Mercy, Depeche Mode and Nine Inch Nails all absorbed its sonic DNA. It would become a cornerstone of post-punk, industrial and gothic rock. Ian Curtis reportedly played *The Idiot* in his final hours. Nick Rhodes from Duran Duran called it a masterpiece, and Siouxsie Sioux saw it as proof of Iggy's genius. Still, the album's architecture bore Bowie's fingerprint throughout. 'There was a power to the music he was willing to provide for me', Iggy reflected in *Mojo* in 2012. 'It was perfect, and I loved it.' Bowie had built a world in which Iggy could re-emerge: corroded, dissonant and newly modern.

Upon release, Iggy described his new sound to *NME* as 'a cross between James Brown and Kraftwerk', calling it his 'album of freedom'. For Bowie, it was a trial run for what came next. To avoid any impression of artistic derivation, *The Idiot*'s release was strategically delayed, as Bowie was about to begin work on a new album in a similarly experimental vein. He returned to the Château in September and began work on what would become one of the defining achievements of his career. Using *The Idiot* as a departure point, he aimed to rewrite his own musical language without the confines of his past success. 'I wanted to move out of the area of narrative and character; I wanted generally to reevaluate what I was doing', he told *Melody Maker* in 1977. 'I was afraid that if I continued to work in that environment, I would begin repeating myself. I felt that that was the way I was heading.'

Looking to experiment with new ways of writing and recording music, he reached out to Brian Eno. By then, Eno had already charted his own path from glam provocateur to avant-garde visionary. After leaving Roxy Music in 1973, he released a series of increasingly idiosyncratic solo albums, blending glam, art rock and avant-pop irreverence, before gradually shifting towards instrumental works shaped by generative systems and mood. This evolution culminated in *Another Green World*, *Discreet Music* and *Evening Star*, a collaboration with King Crimson guitarist Robert Fripp, albums that distilled his new approach: spare in form, guided by process and animated by atmosphere rather than structure. Bowie sensed it could unlock something. Speaking to *NME* in 1979, he reflected on Eno's approach:

> He's the kind of person who doesn't define himself as a musician, but rather, he is more interested in concepts and methodologies instead. For him, I suppose, the synthesiser is one of the perfect instruments for practices like scientific experiments.

One day during the early sessions for Ultravox's debut album, co-produced by Eno, he told the band that Bowie had phoned him, wanting to collaborate on a new record. 'He wasn't sure whether it was the right thing for him to do, thought it might be too commercial or too pop,' John Foxx recalled in the 2014 BBC Radio 4 documentary *Bowie In Berlin*, 'and we all said: 'Go on, you've got to do it. Bowie is great. It'd be fantastic." Soon after that push, Eno packed his EMS Synthi AKS and left for the sessions that would become *Low*.

A mini modular analogue synthesiser built into a briefcase, the Synthi was designed for portability and creative control. Unlike the large and unwieldy Moogs of the early 1970s, it was compact, versatile and could be paired with a keyboard, making it ideal for musicians who were used to composing at the piano. This kind of EMS technology had already found its way into the work of Kraftwerk and Tangerine Dream, and into Eno's own recordings: with Roxy Music, in solo ambient pieces and during his recent sessions with Harmonia, where he worked with a related VCS3 model.

With Eno just as infatuated as Bowie with the German experimental scene, the *Low* sessions drew from their shared interest in abstraction, repetition and texture. The core group for the album's snappy art-funk side once again included the DAM trio, now joined by Roy Young, former keyboardist with The Rebel Rousers, and Ricky Gardiner, the guitarist from Beggars Opera. Bowie played guitar, saxophone, piano, vibraphone, xylophone, harmonica and a range of synthesisers. Eno, who joined the sessions later, took charge of the Minimoog, EMS Synthi, ARP synthesiser, Chamberlin and piano, adding vocal treatments and guitar processing along the way. Among the guests during the Château sessions was Mary Hopkin, then married to producer Visconti, who was now back at the controls. She contributed backing vocals to 'Sound And Vision', a fragmentary snapshot of the aftermath of Bowie's worn-out, darker days in LA. He told *Q* in 2003:

> *Low* was largely drug-free. That was the first instance in a very long time that I'd gone into an album without anything like that to help me along. I was scared because I thought that maybe my creativity had to be bound up with drugs – that it enhanced my ability to make music. But that album turned out okay.

Low Profile

Low clicks on mid-transmission, the signal already live. 'Speed Of Life' began as a vocal track, but Bowie, caught in a creative freeze, left it unwritten. Its unfinished state leaves it open-ended, unresolved and elusive. It marks Bowie's first released instrumental, a bold step into purely musical expression, its title apparently alluding to the Tree of Life.

The result is a fragment in motion: coiling guitar figures, ARP arpeggios and a darting, descending synthesiser motif first heard in 'The Laughing Gnome' and 'Fame', and later recurring across Bowie's work, from 'Scream Like A Baby' to 'Scary Monsters' and 'The Last Thing You Should Do'. Bass and drums dominate the mix, forming a demanding funk rhythm chassis over which distortion, noise and synthetic textures writhe. The structure doesn't unfold but revolves, built from distinct sections that operate independently rather than driving toward resolution. Bowie had initially imagined them as a coherent whole until Eno suggested retaining their strangeness by leaving them separate.

Most striking is the drum sound: a processed, destabilised force that became one of the album's most enduring sonic signatures. The effect was created using the Eventide Harmonizer H910. Although Maslin had already used the device on *Station To Station*, and it had been tested during the making of *The Idiot*, Visconti's experiments pushed it further. On a conference call before the sessions began, when Bowie and Eno asked what it would do, Visconti gave his now-famous reply: 'It fucks with the fabric of time.'

The machine could shift pitch without affecting speed and responded to the intensity of the input signal, meaning Davis could actively shape the sound as he played, controlling the resonance of each hit in real time. The result wasn't mixed in afterwards but captured live, making it all the more difficult to replicate. That warped temporal quality, producing the snare's distinctive falling cascade, defines not only 'Speed Of Life' but the whole of side one. In the 2018 video series *Tracing My Dad*, Visconti estimated that Davis contributed around 60% of that side's sound, adding that he created effects 'no one in the world had heard yet'.

Although clearly touched by a wider current of German experimentalism, *Low* is still routinely linked to Kraftwerk. Bowie later stressed a key difference: 'Kraftwerk's percussion sound was produced electronically, rigid in tempo, unmoving. Ours was the mangled treatment of a powerfully emotive drummer, Dennis Davis. The tempo not only 'moved' but also was expressed in more than 'human' fashion', he told *Uncut* in 1999. He also emphasised that, unlike Kraftwerk's meticulously planned compositions, the music on *Low* 'was spontaneous for the most part and created in the studio.'

'Speed Of Life' exemplifies the first side of the album as the collision of two forces: a tightly drilled R&B-rooted rhythm section and stark electronics shaped by synthesisers, deformed guitar tones and a broader absorption of Germany's avant-garde. The combination felt genuinely new, even to those involved. The sound stood apart from anything Bowie had recorded up to that point: alien, uncompromising and operating in an entirely different register, innovative yet strangely timeless. Most of the tracks on side one drift in and out without clear beginnings or endings. They feel suspended in the listening experience, as if their length could be stretched or cut off at any point. Where lyrics appear, they are rarely the focus. Rather than presenting the artist as a solitary figure struck by inspiration, the album shows Bowie as a gravitational centre, drawing in collaborators and influences to create something larger than any single hand.

That openness is echoed in the structure of side one. Rather than flowing as a continuous suite, it is cut into short, sharp pieces that break off as suddenly as they begin. Hooks surface and vanish, melodies are hinted at and abandoned, and the cost-efficient lyrics feel more like fragments of thought than declarations. The album contains fewer words than any of Bowie's earlier records: the whole of *Low* could fit in 'Cygnet Committee' alone. He utters them in a flat, detached delivery. The effect is volatile yet cohesive: a mosaic of half-finished gestures that together capture Bowie's unsettled state of mind. 'A dreadful state really', he told *Q* in 1989.

In those fragments, Bowie sketches vignettes of isolation and psychic disintegration: loneliness, numbness and emotional retreat. An undercurrent of autobiography pulses beneath the stark, cypher-like phrases he permits himself to voice on side one. During the sessions, he had to leave to deal with a custody dispute with Angie and to attend a court hearing in the legal battle with his former manager, Michael Lippman, who had succeeded Defries. 'He was away for about four days in Paris, dealing with this deposition,' Visconti told *Melody Maker* in 1977, 'and he was absolutely down for that month.' One night at the Château, Angie arrived with her then-boyfriend, sparking a fierce argument that fed into the raw nerve of 'Breaking Glass', a song that also hints at occult and Kabbalistic symbolism from Bowie's coked-out Duke rite. Asked about it in 1999, he told *Uncut*: 'A contrived image, yes. It refers to both the Kabbalistic drawings of the Tree of Life and the conjuring of spirits.'

'What In The World' began as a leftover from *The Idiot*, shaped by Iggy's backing vocal and a lyric tracing emotional isolation and frayed intimacy, with the hidden anima at its core. Jittery, chaotic and bristling with competing signals, the song becomes a scrambled love song haunted by disconnection, sensory overload and collapse of meaning.

Among the album's highlights, 'Sound And Vision' showcases Bowie's eclecticism: a Bo Diddley-style groove entwined with shimmering synths that echo the lush, melody-driven sound of a Mantovani-inspired 101 Strings Orchestra, forming a sublime hymn to stasis, creative paralysis and detachment. 'A very sad song for me', Bowie recalled in *Q* in 2003. 'It was the first time I knew I was killing myself and time to do something about my physical condition. I had a few scares and thought, 'Well, I got through that by the skin of my teeth.' Serious haemorrhaging from the nose, passing out … awful stuff.'

'Always Crashing In The Same Car' was inspired by another bleak episode, according to Bowie. On the Kurfürstendamm in Berlin, he had spotted the coke dealer he believed had ripped him off and gave chase in his rusty open-top Mercedes – a gift from Iggy and Coco – repeatedly smashing into the car. 'He looked around every second, and I could see he was mortally terrified for his life', Bowie told the audience at the BBC Radio Theatre in 2000. 'I rammed him for a good five to ten minutes. Nobody stopped me. Nobody did anything.' Later that night, he circled the hotel garage with his foot jammed on the accelerator, reaching a kind of spiritual impasse as he considered letting go. At that precise moment, the engine gave out. What followed was not a crash, but the most subdued track on side one: a rumination on inner doubt and self-reproach, drifting in a haze of trance and listless inertia, ending in a wordless cry before Gardiner's keening solo cuts through.

Young's boogie-woogie chops are used to great effect in 'Be My Wife', a propulsive, piano-driven track with Bowie's vocals once again confined to an affectless, weary range. Its title may nod to Nina Simone's 'Be My Husband', yet lyrically it questions the very act of expressing love, simultaneously pleading, ironic and emotionally spent, closing the vocal section of side one with Bowie at his most enigmatic and ambivalent. The sequence ends with 'A New Career In A New Town', its harmonica-led wistfulness clashing with electronic sonorities, past and future intertwining in fragmentary, cyclical patterns.

From there, side two shifts decisively away from rock song form, trading guitars and hooks for spacious semi-instrumentals built by Bowie and Eno around atmosphere and tonal detail. Eno described them as 'non-songs'. The undercooled anxiety of side one gives way to a pensive, slow-shifting minimalist logic, echoing Cluster, Reich and Glass through looping motifs, modular repetition and long-form decay. These pieces don't narrate, but they evoke: East Bloc isolation, dying grandeur, voices dissolving into static.

The results are stark and immersive. 'Warszawa' unfolds over solemn, unrelenting piano chords, soon enveloped by synth layers and an invented Slavic vocal. 'Art Decade', rescued from the outtakes pile by Eno, moves through two interlocking sections of melancholic, repeating melodies, with cello by Hansa engineer Eduard Meyer, conjuring a funereal portrait of West Berlin: a fading city, isolated from its art, culture and vitality. Recorded solely at Hansa, where the album was completed, 'Weeping Wall' is Bowie's meditation on the Wall's silent suffering, built from layered xylophone, piano and vibraphone over a pulsing synth bed, with wordless vocals dissolving into Chamberlin-tinged textures and touches of distorted guitar colouring its austere minimalism. 'Subterraneans', its title echoing Jack Kerouac's 1958 novel, closes the album in a tone of mournful displacement, written as a lament for those trapped in East Berlin, Bowie's faint jazz saxophone tracing the ghost of a vanished era.

Although Bowie loved the Château for its ramshackle cosiness, the sessions took place in surroundings that were more prosaic than romantic. With most of France on holiday, the studio was understaffed and its equipment left to fend for itself. Each morning, Visconti had to recalibrate the multitrack recorder by hand, guided only by a novice assistant and the manual. Conditions were functional but far from luxurious. Meals were repetitive, mostly rabbit, and late-night requests for food or drink went unanswered until Bowie confronted the Château's owner directly. One night, both he and Visconti fell ill after eating unrefrigerated cheese. When a local doctor refused to examine Visconti on the grounds that he was still mobile, Bowie shared his own medication with him.

Whether it was the cheese or the cure, spectral activity seemed to increase. The corridors were said to echo with the ghosts of Frédéric Chopin and George Sand, and Bowie sensed that the castle carried something unsettling. 'It was a spooky place', he told *Uncut* in 1999. 'I did refuse one bedroom, as it felt impossibly cold in certain areas.' In the same interview, Visconti recalled a corner that seemed to absorb light, describing the bedroom as 'haunted as all fuck'. Eno claimed someone shook him awake every morning, though no one was ever there. His room had once belonged to Chopin, who died of consumption. Eno, too, developed a persistent cough.

Although Bowie had entered the sessions as a creative trial with no fixed outcome, *Low* was completed in just five weeks, conceived from the outset as a radical experiment at a time when no one else was making records like it. 'It was a sort of industrial extrapolation of what was going on in soul and funk records', Eno said on *Totally Wired* in 1987. 'One side was urban and industrial, the other side was suburban. It was the quiet spots in the city.' Bowie, Eno and Visconti worked as a unit, building strange sonic structures and sculpting a quiet revolution, before Bowie and Visconti took over the mixing. Initially titled *New Music: Night And Day*, the album was renamed to reflect both the tone of the songs and the visual pun of its sleeve image from *The Man Who Fell To Earth* – Bowie in low profile. 'David was going through a difficult period professionally and personally. To his credit, he didn't put on a brave face. His music said that he was 'low'', Visconti told *Uncut* in 1999.

Beneath its fractured surface, the album carries a peculiar charge: a tug-of-war between depression and propulsion, bleakness and persistence. As Bowie veered between euphoria and desolation, clawing his way out of psychic freefall, *Low* became an X-ray of that struggle: emotionally disjointed yet edged with a tentative resolve, exposing not just damage but the faint outlines of recovery. Speaking to *Uncut* in 1999, he recalled: 'Overall, I get a sense of real optimism through the veils of despair from *Low*. I can hear myself really struggling to get well.'

After completing the recordings at Hansa, Bowie stayed on in Berlin, soon settling on Hauptstraße 155. A city that would galvanise the atmosphere around him and tune the air towards *"Heroes"*.

Berlinerluft

Berlin had undergone dramatic transformations since becoming the capital of the German Reich in 1871: from the abdication of Kaiser Wilhelm II to the roaring 1920s, marked by sexual freedom and avant-garde experimentation, followed by the rise of Hitler and the Nazis, the devastation of the Second World War and its long shadow. The Cold War began here, and so did the divide.

By the time Bowie settled in Berlin in the autumn of 1976, the city was a walled island in a partitioned world. The concrete barrier that split it in two had stood since 1961, cleaving streets, families and histories into East and West. No longer merely divided into occupation zones, Berlin was now physically and ideologically severed by Cold War imperatives. The Wall ran for over a hundred kilometres, with checkpoints, watchtowers and floodlights serving as daily reminders of global deadlock.

On the western side, Berlin functioned as a capitalist enclave within East German territory, propped up by federal subsidies and loaded with symbolic weight. American, British and French troops remained on alert, a quiet fixture of the Cold War's armed peace and Berlin's precarious NATO status.

Many young men had moved there deliberately to avoid conscription, fuelling an influx of anti-militarist thinkers and alternative lifestyles. In northern Kreuzberg, an underground scene of protest, drugs and activism began to brew. Police raids on occupied buildings sparked tension, and at times, fierce street clashes. Subcultures thrived in backstreets and basement venues, from anarchist squats in Kreuzberg to smoky avant-garde bars in Schöneberg.

East Berlin, by contrast, was the GDR's showpiece capital: tightly managed, heavily monitored. The Stasi's surveillance reached deep into everyday life. Socialist slogans filled the streets, but the economy was strained and the atmosphere brittle. Culture persisted, though under pressure, and cross-border movement remained rare and heavily restricted. Berlin had become a paradox: frozen yet volatile, confined yet creatively restless. Still marked by war, shadowed by politics and braced against opposing futures, the city in 1976 offered no resolution. Only tension, mutation and the faint possibility of transformation.

Birthplace of Marlene Dietrich and Brigitte Helm, and once home to Albert Einstein and Christopher Isherwood, the Schöneberg neighbourhood still carried traces of its bohemian past: late-night cafés, run-down bars and a visible queer community that had weathered years of repression and quiet defiance. Turkish grocers and repair shops had begun to appear along the street, as the area became increasingly shaped by Berlin's immigrant working class. It was a place where the weight of history lingered in the walls.

In the final days of the war, as Berlin collapsed under artillery fire and chaos, a soldier was found hanging from a lamppost, a short walk from the doorway of Bowie's apartment. He was strung up by civilians in reprisal for refusing to fight. A cardboard sign was tied to his braces, reading: 'I, Corporal Höhne from Berlin, was too cowardly to defend my wife and children.' Reported in the Nazi paper *Der Panzerbär* on 25 April 1945, the image captured a city in moral freefall. It was one more trace in a neighbourhood where history pressed in from every side, etched into the cobbles beneath Bowie's feet. 'It's a city that bears the scars of history on its skin, yet it continues to search, to change. There's a strange atmosphere there, suspended between nostalgia and future, decay and rebirth. It's a stimulating place', Bowie told *Ciao 2001* in 1977.

Above a car parts shop at Hauptstraße 155, behind the door of an unassuming apartment block, lay a spacious seven-room flat with high ceilings and Art Deco-framed windows. The dark, wood-panelled interior and parquet floors were austere, functioning more like a dormitory-cum-garret than a home. Coco occupied a separate apartment within the flat, Iggy had a room of his own and Bowie lived among them with Zowie and his nanny occasionally in tow. His own quarters were more indulgent: furnished with Tiffany lamps, heavy drapery, Brücke-style expressionist portraits, richly woven rugs and a wood-burning fireplace, it was the most lavish space in the apartment. One room was set aside as a painting studio, crammed with easels, canvases, brushes and books on the German Expressionists he studied and collected.

Bowie and Iggy's domestic life had the texture of a lopsided camaraderie, half play and half rivalry. 'Who did the chores? Well, I seem to remember doing a little hoovering', Iggy told *Q* in 2008. 'The big event of the week was Thursday night. Anyone who was still alive and able to crawl to the sofa would watch *Starsky & Hutch*.' Bowie remembered in *Der Tagesspiegel* in 2002:

> Our daily routines were quite opposite. And Iggy would always devour anything he could find in the fridge, which really got on my nerves. I was the one who did the grocery shopping, and he'd eat everything up. Sometimes, I'd treat myself to some really tasty stuff, like when I went to KaDeWe's gourmet floor, but a few hours later, it was all gone again. It drove me nuts. So, he moved out and got an apartment in the same building, directly across from mine.

Breakfast often meant a stop at Anderes Ufer, the café a few steps from their front door. Unlike most gay bars in the city, which were tucked away from sight, this one had windows facing the street, a small act of boldness that gave it a certain notoriety. When vandals once shattered the glass with a brick, Bowie covered the repairs out of his own pocket. Their Berlin routines were subdued compared to the drug-fuelled delirium of LA, yet sobriety was never really on the menu. Nights out meant drinking KöPi at Joe's Bierhaus or Paris Bar, stopping by the cabaret drag bar The Lützower Lampe, or a late descent into Schöneberg's nightclub haze. 'If there wasn't enough to do, I knew some bad people, and I'd get stoned or drunk', Iggy told *Blender* in 2003. 'Sometimes I'd do the bad stuff with Bowie, and the good stuff with the bad people.' On VH1's *Behind The Music* in 1999, he reduced their weekly rhythm to a terse formula: 'Two days for bingeing for old time's sake; two more days for recovery; and that left three days to do any other activity.'

Together they often took the S-Bahn, which traced an uncanny path: departing from West Berlin, gliding soundlessly through the East, then looping back into the West. They could disembark at a tightly controlled station in East Berlin, buy tax-free cigarettes and bottles of absinthe under the gaze of border guards, and reboard for the return journey. That repetitive movement, the sensation of drifting through zones of surveillance and suspended tension, helped inspire Iggy's lyrics for 'The Passenger'. During the Weimar era, Berlin's reputation for sexual freedom and artistic excess had once prompted the Nazis, in a burst of pseudo-scientific zeal, to blame it all on an alkaline trace in the air: the so-called *Berlinerluft*. One wonders what it did to Iggy, pacing the city for hours, exploring every corner on foot.

For Bowie, Berlin was more than just a backdrop for creative reinvention. It was the jagged spirit of the city, its collisions of old and new, ruin and survival, that mirrored his own internal shift. Berlin nurtured its own bleakness, its greyness, its almost aggressive modernity. But it also offered him the two things he needed most in that moment: freedom and anonymity. He told *Uncut* in 1999 about his decision to move to Berlin:

> Life in LA had left me with an overwhelming sense of foreboding. I had approached the brink of drug-induced calamity one too many times, and it was essential to take some kind of positive action. For many years, Berlin had appealed to me as a sort of sanctuary-like situation. It was one of the few cities where I could move around in virtual anonymity. I was going broke; it was cheap to live. For some reason, Berliners just didn't care. Well, not about an English rock singer anyway.

He spent long hours at the Brücke-Museum, drawn to the raw lines and sombre moods of Kirchner, Schmidt-Rottluff and Heckel, and explored Berlin's contemporary galleries in parallel with the Expressionist tradition that had captivated him. Miles from LA's sunstruck delusion, he began edging toward something resembling ordinary life. He took trips to the Black Forest with Iggy and Coco, lingered over long winter lunches at the Wannsee, shopped at record stalls and flea markets, and spent evenings with intellectuals and beats at the Exil restaurant in Kreuzberg.

'Berlin was the first time in years that I had felt a joy of life and a great feeling of release and healing', he told *Uncut* in 1999. With his hair short, wearing simple jeans, checked shirts and the occasional flat cap, even growing a moustache for a time, he could blend into a city that gave him the space to move freely: passing Brecht's blitzed apartment in Wilmersdorf,

Kirchner's old studio in Steglitz, or cycling on his three-gear Raleigh along the Wall. In 2003, he reflected in *Vogue*: 'When I settled there, I found the claustrophobia of the Wall almost comforting. I agree that at times it was like living in a timeless zone. No English TV to speak of, except AFN, the American Forces Network.' His recent flirtations with fascist rhetoric also began to lose their grip, quietly undercut by the weight of the city's unresolved traumas. Among the grotesque realities he encountered, Bowie was appalled by the orthodontist in his building who kept replica skulls of Hitler's cabinet to demonstrate the dental superiority of 'Nordic blood'. In a 1980 interview with *NME*, he recalled:

> The first thing that happened to me when I got to Berlin was that I really had to face up to it because all the people I had as friends there were naturally extreme leftists. Suddenly, I was in a situation where I was meeting young people of my age whose fathers had actually been SS men. That was a good way to be woken up out of that particular dilemma yeah, I came crashing down to earth when I got back to Europe.

Yet despite his newfound normality, even his 'everyman' persona, though necessary to regain a sense of stability, carried its own quiet theatricality. It was shaped by the Berlin he carried in his mind, by Isherwood's lens, and by his ongoing need to construct new selves and self-mythology. Not everything was an idyllic new start or a redemptive arc. There was the continuing financial and legal fallout with Lippman, including unresolved claims that kept pressing on him. The strain put him on a tight budget, which Coco monitored closely, as she did with Iggy's spending. Tension in his marriage to Angie and disputes over their son weighed on him. Cutting back on cocaine merely redirected his excesses into whiskey, brandy and large German beers, pushing him further toward alcoholism. 'I went from drugs into an alcohol stage', he told the *LA Times* in 1993. 'For a while one feels, 'Ah, I've kicked drugs.' But what I discovered was I had another addiction instead.' Hardly the wisest time to set off with Iggy Pop and two fellow mercenaries of booze and blow.

Echo Chamber

Not knowing what to make of the clinical depression *Low* delivered, RCA deemed it unfit for the Christmas market and delayed its release, fearing it would flop. *Young Americans* and *Station To Station* had been massive commercial hits, and the label wanted more in that vein. But *Low* left them stunned. They rejected the album by telegram, urging Bowie to make a second *Young Americans*. Knowing RCA were contractually obliged to release the record anyway, he refused to make any changes. He later pinned the telegram to his wall at home. His former manager, Defries, also tried to block the release, hoping to protect his royalty settlement after their acrimonious 1975 split.

As the wrangling continued, Bowie turned 30 in Berlin, celebrating with Iggy, Coco and friends at Haag's cabaret club Chez Romy. A week later, *Low* finally appeared, and opinions were split from the start. Although now widely acclaimed as one of Bowie's finest, frequently listed among the greatest albums of all time and credited as a key influence on post-punk, *Low* met with hostility in some quarters on release.

Rolling Stone questioned Bowie's avant-garde ambitions, suggesting he lacked the self-assured humour to pull them off. *Creem* slated the record as 'inaccessible', while *NME* condemned it as 'a state of mind beyond desperation' and 'an act of purest hatred and destructiveness', and asked bluntly: 'Who needs this shit?'

Other responses were more measured. *The Village Voice* initially dismissed side two as 'banal', revising that view six months later, when *Low* seemed 'quite pop, slick and to the point.' *The Guardian* described it as Bowie's 'least commercial' yet 'most experimental' album and *National RockStar* noted it as 'his most bizarre and adventurous LP.'

Praise was no less emphatic. *Melody Maker* dubbed it 'the music of Now' and *ZigZag* 'a gamble which succeeds.' *The New York Times* found it 'alluringly beautiful', among Bowie's finest, while *Sounds* declared it a 'mechanical classic.' *NME*'s second review, published in the same issue as the scathing one, concluded *Low* to be 'the ONLY contemporary rock album.' Despite baffling many, *Low* was still placed in year-end lists by *Sounds*, *NME* and *The Village Voice*.

While reviewers picked sides, listeners turned up. *Low* entered the UK Albums Chart at number 37, then climbed to number two the following week, and stayed on the chart for 30 weeks. Abroad, its chart performance was strikingly strong for a record so experimental: number 11 in the US, top ten in Australia and Norway, and chart entries across Europe, from the Netherlands and Sweden to Austria and Finland. Although RCA had been perplexed by the album, the single 'Sound And Vision' reached number three in the UK, though it stalled at 69 in the US, marking Bowie's commercial downturn there until 1983. The second single, 'Be My Wife', saw no US release and became the first new Bowie track since 'Changes' to miss the UK top 50.

Rather than promote the album with a tour, Bowie chose to join Iggy on *The Idiot Tour* as keyboard player, alongside *Low* guitarist Ricky Gardiner and the Sales brothers, Tony and Hunt, Bowie's future rhythm section in Tin Machine. Rehearsals took place at the former UFA studios in Berlin, once the nerve centre of Goebbels' propaganda empire. The vast building was largely abandoned: crumbling, echoing, its peeling walls and rusted cabinets still filled with Nazi-era paperwork. A grim backdrop for Iggy's first real test as a solo act.

Bowie may have been the biggest name on stage, but he chose to stay in the background, keeping the focus on Iggy and limiting himself to keys. It was a conscious gesture of support, and one he was happy to make: the tour wasn't just about the music, but about giving Iggy the momentum to expand his reach. Bowie's presence remained a rumour until the night before the tour opened. From then on, the audience would gather on the right side of the stage, where he took his place behind his Baldwin and synths, smoking Gitanes. 'It was great not having the pressure of being the singer up front', he told *Q* in 1993. 'The drug use was unbelievable and I knew it was killing me, so that was a difficult side of it.'

The Idiot Tour took Iggy, Bowie, Gardiner and the Sales brothers to six UK dates, three in Canada and 20 across the US, in a run stretching from early March to mid-April 1977. After the well-received shows, a breezy daytime appearance on *Dinah!* and a promotional trip to Japan, they returned to Berlin, fired up to make a second Iggy Pop album with the first freshly released. With some new songs already road-tested, Iggy was ready to bottle that momentum with his tight live outfit at Hansa Studio.

The building at Köthener Straße 38, just across from the Wall, had long been steeped in German history. Located a little over a kilometre from Hitler's former bunker, it stood on ground still heavy with the echoes of the Reich. Built in 1913 as a guild hall for the Berlin Builders' Society, its Meistersaal quickly evolved into a chamber music venue and a lively cultural hub during the Weimar years. The Marxist publisher Malik-Verlag moved in downstairs, Kurt Tucholsky gave readings upstairs and a Dadaist gallery showed works by George Grosz and John Heartfield, both at the core of Berlin's avant-garde. After the Nazi takeover, Malik-Verlag was banned and its books publicly burned. The hall was repurposed for Reichsmusikkammer concerts, where SS officers swayed to regime-approved music, until Allied bombs tore through the rear wing and surrounding blocks in 1943.

In the post-war years, the space briefly operated as a cabaret before sliding into disuse. By 1961, what had once been the heart of Berlin's creative energy now found itself stranded at the edge of the Western sector, pressed up against the newly constructed Wall. Its quiet, undesirable location proved attractive to Ariola Records, who saw potential where others saw dust.

In 1964, the Meistersaal was reborn as a recording venue: first for Ariola Sonopress classical sessions, later for Schlager productions. Two years earlier,

Peter and Thomas Meisel had founded Hansa Records under their publishing firm Edition Meisel & Co. They began using Ariola's studio facilities at Köthener Straße before opening their own Hansa Tonstudio 1 in 1973, located in Halensee, West Berlin. Then in 1975, the brothers took over the Meistersaal space from Ariola and rechristened it Hansa Tonstudio 2, expanding the building to house five studio rooms in total. The setup was solid: high-grade equipment, resonant acoustics and a proven track record with operas, soundtracks and Schlager. When a genuine superstar like David Bowie arrived in 1976, it marked a shift in scale that would reframe the studio's legacy. Not that everyone took notice at first. 'I had no idea who he was', Hansa engineer Meyer told *The Berliner* in 2014. 'He was not coming from the stars, we did not roll out a red carpet for him ... he was simply a client of our studio.'

Just outside, the Wall loomed, patrolled by armed guards in watchtowers. Beyond it, the grey void of East Berlin stretched into silence. From the control room window, musicians could see barbed wire, searchlights and concrete, crowding the margins of a tense and brittle city. That tension, that eerie stillness, gave Hansa a charged, haunted allure. The music Bowie would make here, both on his own and with Iggy, would turn the studios into a place of legend, attracting a wave of international artists in search of the same otherworldly magic.

It must have suited Bowie, too. After a first taste during the final *Low* sessions, he now returned with Iggy after *The Idiot Tour*. The weathered building stood quiet and imposing. Its Ionic columns still bearing wartime damage, its upper windows sealed with brick, parts of the structure simply collapsed. From certain windows, one could glimpse the mined strip of death ground and the patrols beyond it. The Wall had become a canvas, covered in spray-painted slogans, bursts of anger, longing, or absurdist wit layered over the concrete. It was a surreal and oppressive backdrop to the sessions unfolding inside, with an atmosphere that was tense, enclosed and competitively energising.

Activity ran at a feverish pace in June at Studio 3, the lower room at Hansa. 'Bowie was tired of spending time on my projects and I think he wanted to get it over with really quickly, so 'Let's just rock and get this guy out of my hair", Iggy told *Uncut* in 2006. *Lust For Life* was recorded and finished within two weeks with the touring band, plus Carlos Alomar, whom Bowie had brought in. Iggy had prepared only fragments of lyrics and essentially improvised at the microphone, with most vocals captured in a single take. Bowie himself had scaled back his role from *The Idiot*, sticking to keyboards, as he had on stage. Yet besides co-producing, he remained the main composer, writing or co-writing seven of the nine songs and adding his unmistakable backing vocals.

The Idiot and *Lust For Life* belong together like night and day: opposites in tone, yet inseparable, best heard as a pair to fully grasp the high-voltage creativity that shaped them. Together with *Low* and *The Idiot*, *Lust For Life* was the third major project Bowie completed in under a year, and one more defining record from an astonishing creative run, filled with timeless, exuberant, infectious rock 'n' roll. Most monstrous of all: the title track. It was born at the Hauptstraße apartment, as the Bowie-Pop duo waited for their weekly dose of *Starsky & Hutch*. Bowie picked up Zowie's ukulele and began strumming along to the Armed Forces Network's interval signal. That peculiar Morse code riff became the song's rumbling backbone. With Bowie's offhand suggestion to name it 'Lust For Life', the blueprint was set.

Upon release, the album suffered from little promotion, and soon its availability was limited as RCA's attention was consumed by Elvis Presley's death three weeks earlier and the catalogue reissues that followed. Even so, it climbed to number 120 on *Billboard* and peaked at number 28 in the UK, where it remained Iggy's highest-charting album until 2016. Bowie revisited *Lust For Life* in 1984 with studio covers of 'Tonight' and 'Neighborhood Threat', and with live performances of the title track during the 1996 *Outside Tour*.

After the *Lust For Life* sessions, Bowie attended the French premiere of *The Man Who Fell To Earth* in Paris with Sydne Rome, gave interviews to the press and appeared on French TV shows, and shot the video for 'Be My Wife', a bizarre masterclass in vacant normality. He then took a brief holiday with Bianca Jagger on the Costa del Sol before returning to Berlin.

Like *The Idiot* before it, *Lust For Life* served as a dry run for Bowie's new record. With the worst of his LA shadows eased on *Low* and by the Berliner rebirth, and a new method of writing in place, he was confident enough to book studio time with only one song prepared, determined to make an album that rocked harder than its predecessor. After his recordings with Cluster in June, Eno was back as a creative partner from the outset, the DAM trio once again provided the backbone, Visconti controlled the desk and guitar virtuoso Robert Fripp was about to pick up the phone. In the cavernous Meistersaal at Hansa, Bowie was set to unleash his voice, igniting an album with expressionistic force and art rock intensity.

Words From The Wings

'There was a lot of enthusiasm on *"Heroes"* because Brian and I liked so much of what we'd done on *Low*', Bowie told CBC in 1977. 'We knew we had it in us to do another one.' Their second collaboration adopted the same working method: backing tracks were laid down first, followed by overdubs, with lyrics and vocals coming last. Since *The Idiot*, Bowie had favoured this three-phase process, and he would continue to use it for the rest of his career. Structurally, the album mirrored its predecessor, with a first side built around relatively conventional rock songs and a second dominated by instrumentals. Bowie, who had gained confidence on the piano during his time on the road with Iggy, contributed keyboard parts throughout, along with guitar, saxophone and koto.

The DAM trio spent around ten days in Berlin recording the backing tracks. 'We were so flexible that no matter what he threw at us, we would throw four versions back. And so his ability to decide where he wanted to go could be fashioned immediately with this trio', Alomar told *Forbes* in 2023. 'We had the ability to change in a split, so there was no problem if you wanted to rock 'n' roll or you wanted to go back to being soulful or if you wanted to go electronic, it didn't matter to us because it was all an odyssey.' Murray agreed in *Guitar World* in 2024: 'We nailed it down, kept it going, and we were able to experiment within the rhythmic structure. David was happy with that; it gave him a foundation to lay on whatever else he wanted to lay on top of it, along with Brian.'

By the time the DAM trio had entered Hansa, they were familiar not only with Bowie's compositional approach but also with the presence and input of Eno. A kind of sonic professor with an abstract vocabulary, Eno sometimes spoke in terms that could strike seasoned professionals like Alomar, Murray and Davis as oblique or even pretentious. 'He really isn't a musician as much as he is a technician and an ideas man. He hasn't got super chops, he's got a super concept of controlling and operating synthesisers', Davis said in *Sound International* in 1978. Murray recalled in *Classic Rock* in 2024: 'Whatever the objective was between David and Brian, the direction I took from Brian was challenging, and it took a lot more effort on my part to support it. Not because I didn't like it, but it was foreign to me. It didn't come as naturally as direction from David.' Yet any doubts they initially may have had were outweighed by the results. After hearing the finished tracks on *Low*, they recognised the freshness and excitement of the new direction. 'I didn't really understand how good musicians worked. I'm not a musician myself in that sense', Eno acknowledged in the 2013 BBC documentary *David Bowie: Five Years*. 'When you're working with really great players, like Carlos and Dennis, you have to accept that they have a way of processing that is beyond intellectual.' Still, as he noted, the fusion of their intuitive musicianship with his own input produced something neither side could have arrived at alone. Alomar, at first sceptical, would later echo that view. In *Guitar World* in 2024, he reflected:

> Hearing the finished product of *Low* was definitely surprising. It was so different from anything we had done before. I was very happy with the DAM trio and our offerings. And then I flipped over the album; I just turned off all the lights and got lost in the ambience. It was exciting to hear how our collective efforts resulted in something so groundbreaking.

For Bowie, Eno had opened new doors of perception by treating the studio not as a recording device but as a site for experimentation, process, chance and the creative manipulation of sound. This shift didn't mark Bowie's first break from conventional structure, but deepened his sense of composition as process over outcome, of the studio as a tool for thinking and of music as an emergent space rather than a narrative form. For the new album, he made sure Eno was involved from the very start, sketching ideas together in advance of the band sessions. 'Brian has always worked in a much more cerebral way than I do. He prides himself quite rightly on being an intellectual, whereas I'm far more sorta physical. I sometimes don't know how I come up with some of the things I come up with. With me, it *feels* right; with Brian, he *knows*', Bowie told *The Irish Times* in 1991.

The DAM trio found themselves adjusting from the languid elegance of the Honky Château, where they had spent the previous summer, to the stark surroundings of a decaying studio, dropped into the bare, tense landscape of a concrete island. Alomar recalled in a 2017 interview with Deutschlandfunk:

> The first thing I remember is a soldier at the Wall. We were always in the studio for a very long time, and at some point, someone said, 'Could we open the window and let in some fresh air?' Then the heavy curtains were drawn back, and we looked directly at a watchtower that stood directly opposite the studio behind the Wall. It was very frightening. To the right and left of the tower, two guards with machine guns walked. And one of them suddenly turned around and looked at us closely. Behind him was the death strip and barbed wire, and in the grey fog, the silhouette of gloomy East Berlin.

Visconti was anything but unhappy with the new environment. He told *Sound On Sound* in 2004:

> Working with Bowie is much more than going to a studio; it's a social event, too. We would eat together, go to shows together, go to clubs together and really soak in the local culture. That was always his way of working, and Berlin was perfect for him in terms of what he wanted at that time. It was a stark, scary place, yet it had a very exciting nightlife, with exotic locales such as the Turkish quarter, and it was swarming with artists like Tangerine Dream, who were friends of ours.

Visconti sensed that the sessions and atmosphere around *"Heroes"* were more upbeat and positive than those of *Low*, and told *Uncut* in 1999 that 'the Germans run a studio a hell of a lot better than the French.' He, too, was struck by the Berlin setting:

> The impending danger of the divided military zones, the bizarre nightlife, the extremely traditional restaurants with aproned servers, reminders of Hitler's not too distant presence, a recording studio 500 yards from the Wall: you could've been on the set of *The Prisoner*.

In his 2011 Red Bull Music Academy lecture, Visconti recalled how they passed hulking tanks and black jeeps on their way to the studio, describing the atmosphere as something out of a 'futuristic Arnold Schwarzenegger film'. Crossing into East Berlin felt like stepping 30 years into the past. 'There were no brands, just directives', he said. Billboards showed a bottle of milk or a fish, with slogans like 'Drink milk' or 'Eat fish'. Women walked in beehive hairdos and stiletto heels; the city was locked in stasis. One night, while Bowie sat parked on the West side with a girl, a Red Army soldier knocked on the window asking for a light. 'This guy shouldn't have been in the West', Visconti noted. 'He came under the river in a passage to ask him for a light. David was so freaked out.'

There was comedy, too. 'Once, I made a little joke. I took one of the studio lamps and shone it directly at the guard tower. David and Tony jumped under the table!' Hansa engineer Meyer quipped in *The Berliner* in 2014. Fripp, too, became part of the laughter when he wondered if he was going to get laid in Berlin, using the euphemism, 'I hope I'll wave the sword of union tonight.' 'He'd lay on his Somerset accent extra thick for that. We couldn't stop laughing', Visconti recalled in *Uncut* in 1999. When the sessions dragged, Davis would mime TV shows in front of the CCTV linking studio and control room, cracking everyone up. Eno and Bowie spent entire takes riffing in Peter Cook and Dudley Moore voices. 'Bowie was Pete and I was Dud … It was hilarious. I don't think I've ever laughed so much making a record', Eno told *Uncut* in 2001. 'We certainly had our share of schoolboy giggling fits', Bowie recalled. He was in better condition than he had been in years, both physically and mentally. 'I was eating extremely well as my drug intake was practically zero. I'd start or end the day with a couple of raw eggs and pack in pretty big meals in between. Lots of meat and veg, thanks mum', he told *Uncut* in 1999. Yet a quiet shadow trailed beneath the surface. 'I don't want to put it in some glamorous place', Alomar said in *Mojo* in 2017, reflecting on Bowie's state at the time. 'He was fighting for his marriage, his son; his business was horrible, the touring exhausting and taking every bit of money that he had … Nobody looks at the loneliness.' In the 1999 *Uncut* interview, Bowie suggested that the manic energy of *"Heroes"* still bore traces of *Low*'s unrest. 'It's louder and harder and played with more energy', he observed.

'But lyrically it seems far more psychotic. By now, I was living full-time in Berlin, so my own mood was good. Buoyant even. But those lyrics come from a nook in the unconscious. Still a lot of house cleaning going on, I feel.'

In *NME* in 1977, Eno recalled that the *"Heroes"* sessions were more confused and demanding than those of *Low*. Sessions often ran overnight, leaving him 'in a kind of daze a lot of the time. Days drifting into one another, you know?' A conceptual and process-driven thinker, what struck him most was Bowie's instinctive method in the studio. 'Almost the whole thing was evolved on the spot in the studio. Not only that, everything on the album is a first take! I mean, we did second takes, but they weren't nearly as good.' The tracks came together with startling speed, in sharp contrast to the protracted work Eno had laboured over on *Before And After Science*. 'We had all these backing-tracks very suddenly – it seemed in about two days. And remember: this came after labouring for months and months on my record. And I thought, 'Shit, it can't be this easy." That initial suspicion gave way, in Eno's own words, as things 'gradually began to hang together', especially when Fripp was brought in at short notice to add jagged, layered guitar lines that pushed the album's sound towards something volatile and gloriously unhinged. In the liner notes to the 2017 box set *A New Career In A New Town*, Visconti recalled:

> Carlos, George and Dennis instinctively knew what to do from the start, but played harder than on the previous album. *Low* was like learning a new alphabet. *"Heroes"* was the subsequent pulp fiction novel! Like *Low*, it didn't take very long to record the seven band tracks. They took less than a week. Carlos stayed behind to add more guitar, but the parts were more supportive than fiery. We were expecting Robert Fripp to start the fire.

Reflecting on the sessions, Fripp drew a striking parallel between mid-1970s Berlin, 1960s London and the downtown New York of the early 1980s. In each, he sensed a moment of rupture: control slipping, order breaking down and a volatile space opening up for radical art. 'It's as if the spirit descends and a place, for whatever juxtaposition of reasons, has power', he told *Q* in 2023.

As on *Low*, Bowie left lyrics and vocals until the final stage of the process. Talking about his continued use of the cut-up technique, he told Alan Yentob in *Changes At 50* in 1997: 'If you put three or four dissociated ideas together and create awkward relationships with them, the unconscious intelligence that comes from those pairings is really quite startling sometimes, quite provocative.' Struck by Iggy's off-the-cuff lyricism, he aimed to combine that immediacy with cut-ups as his method on *"Heroes"*, whose lyrics, as he put it in *Musician* in 1983, ended up reflecting 'the street life in Berlin.' A few months after completion, he told *NME*: 'There was no reason why the album should have been called *"Heroes"*. It could have been called *The Sons Of The*

Silent Ages. It was just a collection of stuff that I and Eno and Fripp had put together. Some of the stuff that was left off was very amusing, but this was the best of the batch, the stuff that knocked us out.'

The result is an album powered by a formidable band, laced with experimental, disorienting sonic effects and unexpected turns, with Bowie singing at a ferocity rarely matched, and lyrics that, in all their opacity, open a universe of meanings, references and hidden connections. *"Heroes"* has weight, yet it is laced with a dry wit and a wary sense of release. It's a burst of creative invention: Bowie at full command and intensity, close to fracture, with darkness never far.

The Album

'Beauty And The Beast'

Cabaret chaos: the shudder of the Thin White Duke flickers through a seedy Berlin drag dive, spiralling through distortion and venomous camp, with a buzz saw snarling in the pit. The song opens with spasmodic blips of percussion and synthesiser, an insistent two-note piano, building toms and bass, and Bowie's glissando howl. The intro carries traces of both Neu!'s 1975 track 'Hero' and 'Station To Station', but this time the threat of derailment lingers throughout.

Once the DAM sessions were done, Bowie wanted someone to slash through the tracks, to disrupt, attack and transform the recorded material. Fripp was in New York when Eno and Bowie called from Berlin. 'David said, 'Would you be interested in playing some hairy rock 'n' roll guitar?' I said, 'Well, I haven't really played for three years, but if you're prepared to take a risk, so will I", he recalled in *Classic Rock* in 2015.

A first-class Lufthansa ticket was duly sent. One week later, he boarded his flight to join the *"Heroes"* sessions. At his Frankfurt stopover, his pedalboard, bristling with wires and switches, drew suspicion from customs officers, uneasy amid domestic anxiety over the leftist Rote Armee Fraktion. After landing in Berlin, jet-lagged and sleepless, he checked into his hotel – which he later identified as a former SS headquarters – then took a cab to Hansa, arriving just before six in the evening.

Fripp began his overdubbing blitz that very night. When he asked to hear the songs they wanted him to play on, Bowie declined with a grin, telling him only to play with total abandonment and in a way he would never dare on his own albums. Fripp plugged into Eno's EMS Synthi AKS and reacted live to the tape. 'The very first thing they did was put up 'Beauty And The Beast', and I played straight over it. This is the way I did the rest of the album. They'd put up a track and I'd play. I wouldn't bother rehearsing it. I'd just play', he said in *Melody Maker* in 1979. 'He reacted to each song with little or no direction – and in each case discovered parts and moods not implicit in the music. David, Tony and I watched in awe. I think we were all dazzled', Eno wrote in a 2019 statement to PPL. In the credits of his 1975 album *Another Green World*, Eno had described the sound of his own treated guitars on the track 'Sky Saw' as 'snake guitar' and 'digital guitar'. Fripp's off-kilter tone channels that same warped strangeness, and 'snake guitar' feels like the right tag here. In 2013, the song clearly still did it for him: 'Anyone who's playing 'Beauty And The Beast', you know they get erections', he wryly quipped in the 2013 BBC documentary *David Bowie: Five Years*.

Lifted from the 18th-century fairy tale, where love tames the monstrous and redemption begins with inward grace, the title might suggest candlelit castles and moral awakenings. But Bowie opens 'Beauty And The Beast' with a sneer, not a seduction. He hijacks the familiar and turns it inward, staging a battle within the self. The Beauty is an illusion of control, the Beast a primal hunger that refuses to be bound. In a detached tone, Bowie delivers neurosis, split identities and the creeping sense that someone might not make it out alive.

'Weaving down a byroad, singing the song/That's my kind of highroad gone wrong' signals the descent: already off-track, already unravelling. The lyrics, characteristic of the cut-up method, jump between short phrases and ruptured images, charged with tension through juxtaposition and interruption. Meaning gives way to rhythm and undertow in an anxious psychodrama, where moods, fears and desires collide. Stray interjections such as 'Liebling', 'My-my' and 'Smile at least' lend the track a Weimar-tinged theatricality that blurs the line between irony and sincerity. In the context of the song, Bowie's cry 'someone fetch a priest' evokes spiritual panic, a plea for salvation, an exorcist's call. But the phrase also carries a hidden echo: a censored twist on Visconti's studio catchphrase at the time, 'Someone fuck a priest!', his gleeful outburst whenever a recording hit the mark. A small example of how spontaneity and cut-up fragments can cohere into something oddly potent.

Backing vocals on the track were sung by Antonia Maass, singer with Berlin jazz-rock group The Messengers, with whom Visconti began a discreet fling that summer. Although the story will prove contentious, their now-famous kiss by the Wall is said to have inspired Bowie when writing the title track. In *A New Career In A New Town*, Visconti recalled:

> One night in a club, I heard Antonia Maass singing with her band, and the next day I told David how terrific she was. We tried her out on 'Beauty And The Beast'. David was very impressed. Before long, he had her jumping through hoops (vocal ones), getting her to sing at the very top of her range. He also asked her to sing 'Liebling' as an alternative to 'darling', bringing a little flavour of Berlin into the song.

The classic dichotomy of beauty and beastliness reflects a fractured persona – or indeed Berlin, equally torn: cultured and avant-garde, yet haunted and broken. Watched, surveilled, weighed down by Cold War dread, Berlin hums with unease: 'Something in the night/Something in the day/Nothing is wrong, but darling, something's in the way'. Bowie drifts through the city like a displaced figure, caught between East and West, between curdled dogmas and collapsed ideals. 'There's slaughter in the air/Protest on the wind' hints at coiled tension: RAF bombings, Stasi repression, demonstrations, paranoia. 'Beauty And The Beast' plays out as a psychogeographic snapshot: Berlin's bifurcated surfaces doubling as a broken mirror held up to the former Thin White Duke. Taken as a drug song, echoing LA, it traces the precarious edge between euphoria and collapse. The refrain, 'You can't say no to the Beauty and the Beast', lands with dry resignation, a flat acceptance of an inescapable bind, where craving tips into ruin.

The song's best line, 'Someone else inside me/Someone could get skinned', is laced with both physical violence and the psychic stripping of identity. It recalls the world of *Die Brücke*, with its expressionist distortion of the body and splintered sense of self. Most vividly, it echoes Kirchner's *Selbstbildnis Als Soldat* (1915), where the artist's painting hand has been violently cut off. The canvas turns skin into a site of rupture, both a barrier and a threatened surface. Bowie distils it into language: the human becomes grimace, a nervous carcass stranded in the wrong world. This is subject-becomes-predicate *pur sang*. The psyche is no longer the vessel. It's the scene of the crime.

In the middle-eight, the song suddenly breaks open: the chords shift, Bowie's voice lifts and the production widens the frame. What follows is a fraught admission, driven by a guilt-laced longing for control:

I wanted to believe me
I wanted to be good
I wanted no distractions
Like every good boy should

The effect borders on theatrical: the speaker is both the liar and the one who falls for it. It's a turning point, a bruised moment of self-revelation that makes everything around it feel even more bitter. Bowie's dramatically emphatic vocal delivery contrasts starkly with the cooler, more impassive tone heard elsewhere in the song. It heightens the sense that, for a moment, the 'real person' is speaking, or something close to it, before the final line slips back into mockery, tinged with sarcasm and chased by the return of the relentless, grimy groove. The lines find an echo in 'The Wedding Song' on *Black Tie White Noise*: 'I'm gonna be so good, just like a good boy should'. In 1977, it is a confession in which the monster owns up to having wanted something better, despite knowing he'd only ever be pretending. By 1993, the irony was gone. It is a heartfelt vow to his wife, and just as much to himself. May the beasts rest in peace, stilled by the grace of his 'angel for life'.

On *Musikladen Extra* in 1978, Bowie euphemistically called 'Beauty And The Beast' 'somewhat schizophrenic in nature'. Over a decade later, 'You Can't Talk' from *Tin Machine II* opens with a direct nod: 'Beauty shrieks 'Beast in booties''. Both songs deal with mental disarray, but 'You Can't Talk' breaks down further in its syntax, less theatrical performance, more symptom, in a track that registers more as spasm than song.

'Beauty And The Beast', backed with 'Sense Of Doubt', was released as the album's second single and follow-up to the title track in early 1978. By then, disco was dominating the clubs in the US and powering mainstream pop, while in the UK it was gaining momentum in the singles charts. Punk had exploded in 1977 and, though still present, was already beginning to fracture. In a chart dominated by Wings, Bonnie Tyler and The Bee Gees, Bowie's mongrel-disco hybrid stalled at number 39 and dropped out after three weeks. In the US, it failed to chart altogether. Then again, it's the kind of track that resists accessibility. It lacks melodic pull, the 'My-my' can grate and Fripp's guitar scrapes against any desire to hum along like it's 'Starman'. The song carried funk and bite during the 1978 *Isolar II Tour*, also known as the *Low/"Heroes" Tour* or *Stage Tour*, before Bowie dropped it from his repertoire. Its definitive role remains as the album's opener, where it finds its place in the Berlin gloom, setting the stage for what follows.

'Joe The Lion'

The album really kicks into gear with this engine-revving slab of sonic menace, bursting out with lunging urgency and barely contained ferocity. Fripp's guitar crashes in, then lurches through the track shrieking, stuttering, swerving like a battered engine redlining into a blind curve, driven by death-defying mania. In its wake, Davis ramps up the tension with pounding toms, then locks into a rigid, unflinching beat that nails it to the floor. Alomar's terse, insistent motif jabs and recoils like a plugged-in nerve, taut with distortion and prone to snap. Bowie tears through it all, the introspective restraint of *Low* hurled out the window. He sounds possessed, veering from sneering screams to strangled yelps, pushed to the front with near-desperate intensity. The result doesn't just rock. It snarls and threatens. 'A very aggressive song', Visconti said during Brooklyn Talks in 2018.

Fripp's contribution came from a near-total carte blanche. Bowie told *International Musician* in 1991 that he had barely given him any direction:

> The only premise that I gave him was to play with total abandonment, and in a way that he would never consider playing on his own albums. I said play like Albert King, and he would look puzzled for a few moments, and then he'd go in and try his damnest to get somewhere near it, but it would come out his way. So things like 'Joe The Lion' were him really having a bash at the blues. He was great like that – he really got into the swing of it.

'Joe The Lion' was the first track for which Bowie improvised the lyrics on the spot in the studio. Visconti recalled in *A New Career In A New Town*:

> The first time I heard the vocal was when he asked me to roll the tape. I wasn't expecting the ferocity of the first three words, 'Joe … the Lion' – I almost leapt out of my seat. It was always exciting when, finally, David said he'd written the song! After a couple of additional scribbles on the lyric page and drop-ins on the tape, we had a lead vocal. It took about half an hour.

Bowie described the method to *Uncut* in 1999:

> I would put the headphones on, stand at the mic, listen to a verse, jot down some key words that came into mind, then take. Then I would repeat the same process for the next section, etc. It was something that I learnt from

working with Iggy, and I thought a very effective way of breaking normality in the lyric.

He doubled certain words and phrases directly after recording the lead vocal. After a few playbacks in the control room, he brought in Visconti to add backing vocals. With Visconti singing falsetto, they gathered around one microphone and improvised harmonies, injecting the track with seemingly random stabs that snapped into place with offbeat logic. Their punchy 'yeah yeah's would later return, reshaped, in 'Up The Hill Backwards' in 1980.

Beyond the visceral energy and improvisation lies a striking reference point: 'Joe The Lion' draws on the work of American performance artist Chris Burden, whose staged acts of self-harm and ritual violence fascinated Bowie. He had already encountered Burden's work during his time in LA in 1975, when Burden smuggled his video pieces onto local television by buying commercial airtime. During the *"Heroes"* sessions, Burden was exhibiting at Documenta 6 in Kassel, West Germany, one of the most prominent contemporary art shows in the world, widely covered in the international press. Bowie may have been reminded of Burden through this exposure, through Berlin gallery circles, or even by chance, via a stray article in the studio. Such an encounter would have been a fitting spark for a lyric written on impulse.

Another breadcrumb trail to Burden's work leads through Laurie Anderson, who also exhibited at Documenta 6. Later that same year, she would reference his performance *Shoot* in her composition 'It's Not The Bullet That Kills You (It's The Hole)', four years before her breakthrough with 'O Superman', covered by Bowie on the *Earthling Tour* in 1997. Anderson went on to become an internationally recognised avant-garde artist and the wife of Lou Reed. His Velvet Underground track 'White Light/White Heat' lent its title to one of Burden's most extreme works: a 22-day endurance piece staged in 1975, during which he fasted on a raised platform in the corner of a gallery, completely out of view of the audience. Bowie, who returned to 'White Light/ White Heat' throughout his live career, might have followed the title straight to Burden.

The groundbreaking artist had made his name with a series of such extreme performances that pushed the limits of art, danger and physical resilience. His work veered between control and vulnerability, often blurring the line between spectacle and trauma. In the early 1970s, he locked himself inside a student locker for five days, fired shots at a passing Boeing 747 and lay bolted to a gallery floor beside two buckets of water, each wired with live 110-volt current. In these performances, personal risk and physical ordeal were elevated to artistic principle, forcing performance art into direct confrontation with real consequences.

For 'Joe The Lion', Bowie channels one of Burden's most cited and disturbing works, *Trans-Fixed* (1974), in which he lay face up on a Volkswagen Beetle, his hands nailed to the metal as if crucified on the car. As so often in Bowie's tangled world of strange grafts, even the car seemed to nod to the album's Teutonic mood, as if he invited these curious echoes himself. *Shoot* (1971) also hovers in the background: a performance in which Burden stood motionless in a gallery while a friend shot him in the left arm with a .22 calibre rifle from a distance of 15 feet, captured on 16mm film.

Joe's Bierhaus in Berlin, one of Bowie and Iggy's haunts, may well have lent the song its troubled namesake, while his surname harks back to an earlier idea: 'Magge The Lion', a character name Bowie scribbled on a concept art page for his abandoned *Diamond Dogs* film project in 1974. Joe the Lion is a fractured proxy, part echo of Burden, part provocateur, trying to feel himself through pain as revelation, irony and weary escapism. Bowie's lyrics move between sadomasochistic provocation, dream logic and a kind of performance psychosis. In the ripping opening verse, Bowie transforms *Trans-Fixed* into a post-Beat, sarcastic little play, casting Joe as a barfly-prophet peddling insight for pain: 'Tell you who you are if you nail me to my car'. It rings out as religious crucifixion, rock 'n' roll pose and sick showbiz bargain all at once. Where bodily self-sacrifice in Burden's work served as a path to heightened awareness, here it becomes a *martyrtainment* transaction. Whether Joe has anything to reveal is doubtful, but bluffing and half-drunk, he poses as a fortune teller and turns his body into a grotesque condition, a baited hook with nothing on the line. It sets the tone for the rest of the song: psychologically layered and utterly absurd.

In 'Boy/Thanks for hesitating/This is the kiss off', there's distance, sarcasm, disappointment: hesitation means missing the spectacle. Joe's messiah complex runs on surrender, not nuance. He sneers from the stage he's built: the deal is off, and the rejection is his to deliver. 'Thanks for hesitating' lands with a shrug and a smirk. 'You'll never know the real story' isn't just a dismissal; it's an assertion of control. You had your chance. Now it's too late. Joe backpedals into contempt. Maybe it was only 'just a couple of dreams' he was offering, nothing serious. After all, the addressee barely lives: get up, sleep, repeat. There's nothing to reveal when the life in question is already vacant. 'You can buy God', he blusters, as if selling one last illusion.

Then the floor drops. Flat, resigned, almost bored: 'It's Monday'. The divine offer collapses into a weekday. It's anti-transcendence, a fall from the mythic to the mundane. 'You slither down the greasy pipe', faintly echoing 'Diamond Dogs' with its rope descents into ruin, evokes a pitiful slide: furtive and slightly humiliating. It's followed by another strained motion in the same zombified pattern, delivered with a shaky, off-balance air: 'Hobble over any freeway'. The 'you' of earlier verses starts to blur and the voice turns more reflexive, perhaps even introspective. Joe's swaggering pose begins to crumble. He may now be speaking just as much about himself and the drab, disenchanted life he can no longer fully claim as his own.

A surreal jolt cuts through, 'You will be like your DREAAAMS tonight': an ecstatic cry, drawn out, exaggerated. Suddenly, it sounds as if Joe, back in the saddle of the action hero, is promising a vision or receiving one. It is unclear whether it signals hope or horror, but it is unmistakably possessed. Bowie sings it piercingly, hoarse, immediately followed by grinding, reverberating chords and Davis locking back into the groove. A magical moment on the album. That sonic rupture between the numbed-out routine and sudden exaltation marks the moment Joe briefly reclaims his own myth, just before it slips back into anaesthesia. The song's bleakest punchline arrives with a nod to *Shoot*: 'Guess you'll buy a gun/You'll buy it secondhand'. It sounds like bitter advice to a failed rebel, or perhaps Joe himself is suggesting that, for some sleepwalkers, ending it might be the only way out. The word 'secondhand' gives the gun extra weight: not new or heroic, but used, passed on and already carrying a history. The line creates a miniature narrative, dense with implication.

Bowie ends with the repeated mock-heroic mantra 'Joe the lion, made of iron', like a gorilla thumping its chest. A battle cry, a mask, a warning. Joe is I-R-O-N: unyielding, but also cold and hollow. A self-declared identity in a world without anchors. Joe is left as an avatar of pain, strength and absence. With just a touch of megalomania.

To most listeners, the song's symbolic menace and theatrical unease must have felt even more cryptic at the time, without Burden as a well-known context. Though Burden had taken part in Documenta 6, he was far from a household name in 1977. His notoriety remained largely confined to avant-garde circles, with works like *Shoot* and *Trans-Fixed* known chiefly through sparse documentation and whispered legend. Bowie's allusion would likely have been legible mainly to listeners already versed in performance art, rather than to the broader audience hearing the song at the time.

Bowie's fascination with bodily harm and ritual performance would echo throughout his later work. In 1993, he covered 'Nite Flights' for *Black Tie White Noise*, the title track of The Walker Brothers' 1978 album, which was itself directly inspired by *"Heroes"*. The lyrics conjure images of torn stitches, choking on a 'raw meat fist', and a sense of danger running through cold, subterranean tunnels: a visceral tableau of dread and decay that aligns with Bowie's interest in physical extremity and psychological disintegration. That same year, in the liner notes for *The Buddha Of Suburbia*, he reflected on the limitations of linear storytelling in music and acknowledged that his writing had too often relied on chaos and violence as a 'soft option' to address spiritual and emotional starvation. That self-reflection, alongside his choice of 'Nite Flights', points towards the underworld of *1.Outside*, his criminally underrated 1995 album. Here, murder becomes art and body modification becomes ritual, all set against a backdrop of millennial anxiety and the crumbling structures of late 20th-century society. Subtitled *The Ritual Art-Murder Of Baby Grace Blue: A Non-Linear Gothic Drama Hyper-Cycle*, this fusion of paganism and corporeal excess permeates the music, lyrics, visuals and live presentation.

In the album's 'diary entries', Bowie expanded on the concept of ritual art, linking flesh-based performance to a quasi-sacrificial, blood-obsessed aesthetic. With arch dark relish, he referenced the 'Viennese Castrationists' of the 1970s. The phrase was his pointed label for a Viennese Actionist group notorious for acts of self-mutilation as spiritual or political provocation. He also cited Hermann Nitsch, a member of the group whose work staged animal entrails and bloodletting as ceremonial theatre. 'Public revulsion put the lid on that episode,' Bowie wrote, 'but you can't keep a good ghoul down.'

He went on to draw in Burden's notorious works, including *Trans-Fixed*, as well as Ron Athey, whose practice also involved subjecting himself to pain and evoking death. In *Martyrs & Saints* (1992), part of his *Torture Trilogy*, Athey made incisions in his own body, sometimes using meat hooks and branding, while in *Four Scenes In A Harsh Life* (1994), he incorporated blood-soaked paper towels into the performance.

In interviews from the *Outside* era, Bowie traced the rise of piercing, tattooing and scarification in 1990s Western culture to the decline of the Judeo-Christian moral framework, which had long shaped ideas of virtue, sin and the body. He interpreted them as neo-pagan rituals, signs of a new tribalism attempting to fill a spiritual void. By linking body modification culture to the 'ritual art' of Burden and Athey, he implicitly challenged the boundary between accepted modification, pathological self-harm and public spectacle. On *Outside*, this tension is dramatised in the narrative itself: detective Nathan Adler must determine whether a brutalised corpse is the product of art or murder, echoing Thomas De Quincey's 1827 essay *On Murder Considered As One Of The Fine Arts*. The underlying dilemma is clear: what are we willing to sanctify as meaningful ritual, and when does expression become transgression?

On *Blackstar* in 2016, performance becomes the body in extremis. Where Burden and Athey sought out physical pain, Bowie presented a different threshold: the body as a decaying artefact. Flesh, in his vision, is not mere framing but an active site of meaning. With *Blackstar*, Bowie delivered a sublime form of terminal body art. In the videos for 'Blackstar' and 'Lazarus', he shows physical frailty: bandaged eyes, trembling hands. He lies in pyjamas on a hospital bed, with a cloth over his eyes as if already halfway gone – not a rock star, but an object, a form in transition. He trades gallery lights for camera and montage, but the principle is unchanged: the performer offers up the physical self for contemplation. Just as Burden and Athey made the body a site of pain, sacrifice and significance, Bowie used himself as a surface upon which dying and resurrection are enacted simultaneously. His compulsive scribbling at the desk and vanishing into a wardrobe mark the earthly ending and the crossing into myth. In the 'Blackstar' video, Major Tom returns as a skeleton, a jewel set in his skull, unearthed and worshipped like a relic. Bowie did not disappear. He transformed: his body as final canvas, his death as *acte de présence*.

'"Heroes"'

Genesis

For the record, butchered edits of '"Heroes"', like the single cut, fall outside this discussion and always will. Misreading the song's undertones isn't much better, though it does place it in intriguing company. 'Born In The U.S.A.', 'Every Breath You Take', 'Who Let The Dogs Out': '"Heroes"' stands in equally misunderstood territory. Its use in sports montages, the London Olympics, glossy TV climaxes, swelling film moments and talent-show finales, dripping with manufactured camaraderie, has cemented its anthemic image. Bowie's performances at Live Aid, The Freddie Mercury Tribute Concert and The Concert for New York City only deepened that association, and for all the right reasons. Yet at its core, '"Heroes"' is a stark, bitter portrait of a doomed relationship, shadowed by alcoholism, strain and a precarious sense of heroism. No matter how overplayed, overused, misused, badly covered, or lazily absorbed into the collective indifference of repetition, it remains, and will forever remain, a king among songs.

Drama radiates from both the Cold War faultline and the lovers themselves: two figures meeting in the grip of division, their kiss set against guards in watchtowers and gunfire overhead. Bowie's majestic delivery builds from restraint to desperation, mirroring the moment's tension. This isn't a fantasy of victory; it's defiance in borrowed time, a fleeting act with the power to echo forever, even as 'We can be heroes' hangs in the air with more irony than triumph.

The song's backstory has often been reduced to a single image: Bowie, from the control room at Hansa, spotting a couple kissing by the Wall. Bowie set the thread in motion immediately after the album's release, describing in *Poste Restante* and *NME* how, during the recording sessions, he would often watch through the window as a boy and a girl from West Berlin met on a bench beneath a guard tower. He suspected they were having an affair and had deliberately chosen that loaded setting. 'The situation that sparked off the whole thing was, I thought, highly ironic', he said, calling it the starting point for his lyric and placing the quotation marks in the title to underline that irony. A year later, in *Rolling Stone*, he reflected on the image again, this time with a touch of amused detachment: 'There are much pleasanter places to meet, so why did they choose the gun turret? I assumed their motive was guilt, thus the act of heroism in facing it. Of course, it could just be my wonderful imagination.'

In the decades that followed, the story would keep changing shape, while the first telling may already have been a creative twist on events, as Bowie had already noted in *Playboy* in 1976, 'I can't keep track of everything I say.' The Wall was about 150 metres from Hansa, and its view from the control room has been debated. Later accounts placed the couple much closer, sharing lunch and a fleeting kiss directly below the studio windows. Visconti would go on to identify them as himself and Maass, explaining that Bowie had covered for him in interviews because he was still married at the time. 'What a discreet dude I am', Bowie responded in *Uncut* in 2001.

Two years later, he confirmed to *Performing Songwriter* that it was indeed watching Visconti and 'a German girl' which had sparked the lyrics. In the *Frankfurter Allgemeine Zeitung* in 2008, though, Maass questioned the timeline and denied it could have been her, which only clouded the story further. By now, the tale features an ever-shifting scene: an unknown couple on a bench by the Wall, a censured pair under Hansa's windows, Maass and Visconti kissing in another timeline and Visconti wheeling a sofa over the Wall for no clear reason, all somehow inspiring the same song.

It has also been suggested that Bowie's relationship with varieté-vamp Romy Haag, owner of Chez Romy, may have played a role in the song's inspiration. 'His record company wanted him to break up with me,' she told *De Volkskrant* in 2019, 'our relationship was not good for his image.' RCA's disapproval supposedly led him to keep it hidden, with '"Heroes"' emerging as a love letter to her. According to this reading, the label, already unsettled by the experimental turn of *Low*, may have feared that a scandal involving a trans lover might jeopardise any hope of reigniting Bowie's momentum in the US. While this interpretation yields a fitting, defiant and even moving reading of the song, and remains powerful for those who embrace it, it seems unlikely that Bowie would have bowed to industry pressure about who he was or wasn't dating. This was, after all, the man behind the groundbreaking 1972 *Melody Maker* interview declaring 'I'm gay', a defining moment in bringing gender fluidity and queer sexuality into the mainstream. And just months before recording '"Heroes"', he had defied RCA, pushing through *Low* despite their desire for another *Young Americans*. Bowie's decision to relocate to Berlin, a city that at that point lay far removed from the commercial centres of Anglo-American pop, also suggests that he had little interest in appeasing label concerns. Opting to join Iggy on *The Idiot Tour* rather than tour *Low* further underscored his disregard for RCA's commercial agenda.

In 2024, BBC Radio 4's *Bowie In Berlin* offered yet another take on the origins of the 'Wall couple' story, shaped by the memories of British artist Clare Shenstone, a long-time friend of Bowie. Once the face of Andy Warhol's 1966 UK release of *Chelsea Girls*, she met him a few years later in London. He confided in her when his father died, she comforted him, and she was a last-minute witness at his wedding to Angie in 1970. They remained close, and Shenstone visited him in Berlin at his invitation.

In the documentary, she recalls a day spent walking together, passing Checkpoint Charlie into East Berlin to visit Bebelplatz and the Tomb of the Unknown Soldier, before sharing a kiss by the Wall. 'There were spotlights, and you could see the sentries, and the guns silhouetted. We were holding hands, and he took my other hand and kissed me. It was so beautiful.' She also remembers telling Bowie about a dream in which she swam with dolphins, an image that would resurface in the lyrics as one of the song's most recognisable lines.

The couplet has also been read as a nod to Bowie's inability to swim at the time, but is more directly tied to *A Grave For A Dolphin*, a 1956 novel by Alberto Denti di Pirajno, listed among Bowie's 100 favourite books. In the foreword to Iman's 2001 volume *I Am Iman*, he described it as 'a magical and beautiful love story' that had in part inspired the song. The novel tells the fantastical tale of a doomed love affair between an Italian soldier and a Somali girl, and of the bond she shares with a dolphin. In 1991, Iman and Bowie were even offered the chance to portray the couple in a proposed film adaptation of the story. In a 2021 *Vogue* video, Iman mentioned that she had loved the book long before she met Bowie. The motif crossed into real life when, as a token of his love, Bowie had a dolphin tattooed on his calf.

The origins are secondary to what the song makes of them. In Berlin, as throughout his career, Bowie writes by collage, folding particulars into fiction so that the song reshapes the facts. 'My writing is based on the idea of transience. My writing is a very clear understanding that nothing in this world is a real reality; it is not something that you can hold onto', Bowie told MTV in 1995. The lyrical constructions across *"Heroes"* share structural affinities with the modernist montage of *Berlin Alexanderplatz*, Döblin's 1929 collage of shifting perspectives, songs, headlines and urban noise – another novel Bowie later included in his list of favourite books. Both works present a dislocated inner world shaped by external pressures, where linearity gives way to fragmentation. On the album, characters, scenes and incidents provide the scaffolding: meaning gathers in the gaps, in texture, timbre and atmosphere, in concise motifs and stray images drawn from art, film, literature and private life. Bowie writes through persona, casting himself as observer, creator and narrator – a voice at once staged and felt, stepping in and out of the constructed world, leaving room for the listener to enter. That is why the tale keeps shifting while the work holds firm: '"Heroes"' renews itself whenever you bring your own memories to it. The lovers may change, but the song does not.

From the first bar, it settles into a hypnotic, unyielding groove. '"Heroes"', in fact, was probably the most jammed song on the album,' Visconti recalled in the 2018 video series *Tracing My Dad*, 'these three sections that David and Brian came up with and played over and over again.' Before recording for the album began, Bowie and Eno had spent time sketching basic song structures without lyrics or melodies, shaping the framework that the band would later expand in the studio. Like the other full band pieces on the album, the backbone of what would become the title track was cut live by the DAM trio, with Bowie at the piano. The initial idea stemmed from a chord pattern Bowie had first written for Iggy's 'Success' on *Lust For Life*, which Iggy had gleefully sabotaged. Bowie threw the original sequence to the band, and they ran with it, playing their way into an untitled instrumental that built into a triumphant crescendo. 'It was just two chords', Alomar told *Classic Pop* in 2021. 'I'm thinking like a jazz guy and we don't really have keys, we were like, 'okay, that's 'one', let's go to 'four'', so we'd speak like that.' Speaking to *Uncut* in 1999, Bowie said: 'With such great musicians, the notes were never in doubt. We looked at 'feel' as being the priority.'

The DAM trio locked into a chugging rhythm in the vein of 'Silver Cloud' by La Düsseldorf, the group formed after Neu!, and 'I'm Waiting For The Man', a long-time Bowie touchstone. According to Moby in a 2018 SiriusXM feature, Bowie once revealed to him that '"Heroes"' started out as a cover of The Velvet Underground track before he handed the bare-bones structure to the band. 'That song was like riding a wave … a sonic wave. It just had a beautiful drone that we didn't want to disturb', Alomar told *Guitar World* in 2024. 'My approach was to keep the guitar parts simple yet powerful, allowing David's vocals and the overall production to shine.' Murray's MXR flanger-processed, Motown-flavoured Rickenbacker bassline was doubled by Alomar, while Eno sat in the corner behind his briefcase EMS Synthi, plugged into a Marshall guitar amplifier with four ten-inch speakers, cranked high. Using its joystick, oscillator banks and rotary knobs, he shaped spatial, droning textures and manipulated the guitars by feeding them in as an external source. Calling himself a 'non-musician', a description he once tried to put on his passport, Eno approached the track from angles far outside conventional technique, just as Bowie had anticipated when he decided to work with him. 'Brian had his synths and all kinds of magnetic ribbon things sticking out of it. It was mesmerising', Alomar recalled in *Guitar World*. 'There was leakage all over the microphones,' Visconti noted in *A New Career In A New Town*, 'but it sounded great. Why fix it?'

The live foundation, with its sonic density recalling Phil Spector's Wall of Sound, was down by the time the band wrapped up their part of the sessions. Visconti then edited the eight-minute take to just over six. When work resumed after a week off, Eno set up the EMS Synthi again and, using an oscillator at very low frequency through a noise filter, shaped a pulsating, quivering layer across two tape passes. The resulting atmosphere set the mood and framework for Fripp to push the piece further. Unfamiliar with the track's structure, he unleashed three takes of sustained, spectral lines. Plugged into the EMS Synthi, his 1959 Les Paul produced long feedback notes not with an E-bow, as is still often assumed, but through exact positioning, working with the natural feedback. He knew exactly how far each pitch needed to swell, marking the studio floor with tape to hit every note with precision. As he moved, the sound lingered in the air while Eno reshaped it, adjusting filters and envelopes. In a 1994 interview with *The Mix*, Eno recalled:

> I was sending the guitar to a ring modulator and doubling the frequency of it, pulsing it, filtering it, and all those kinds of things. Fripp himself is very sonically aware, so not everything you hear originates from me, but he would plug into my little synthesiser, and I would play around with his sound.

Visconti assembled the three takes into a composite, bounced-down pair of tracks to manage the 24-track limitations. As he wrote in *Bowie, Bolan And The Brooklyn Boy*:

> This was a challenge in the days before computer-based recording; the concept of cut-and-paste didn't exist. The whole process involved a huge amount of trial and error; we often had to start the two machines at exactly the right moment and freely 'fly' a part from one tape machine to another.

The constant mutation of the three sounds was entirely complementary, their shifting tones and feedback merging into a wailing, weightless guitar line that crowns the song, born of precision, instinct and volume pushed to the edge. 'Fripp's plaintive guitar cry really triggered off something emotive in me', Bowie recalled in archival audio used in *David Bowie: Five Years*. Once the instrumental track was in place, everyone involved knew it was special, with Eno telling *NME* just months later that he immediately had the word 'heroic' in mind even before Bowie wrote a word.

With Bowie's ARP Solina string synthesiser and bursts of Chamberlin brass already in place, further overdubs followed: a tambourine and an improvised cowbell after Bowie spontaneously asked for one but none was at hand. An empty German metal tape reel was used as a substitute, with Visconti and Bowie alternately striking it in Hansa's large room to capture its natural ambience. Although Visconti refers to it in his autobiography as a tape platter, in reference to a 'German recording preference to put a tightly wound reel on an open platter with the top of the tape exposed', it has also been described as an ashtray. Whatever it was, somewhere in the mix, some German-made Hansa property is being bashed.

Bowie left the track untouched for weeks until, one day at Hansa, he started sketching out lyrics, drawing on all kinds of influences, while he may or may not have looked out of a window. 'When I am king, dilly dilly, you shall be queen': the song's first verse echoes this line from the nursery rhyme 'Lavender Blue', whose 1959 US hit version by Sammy Turner was stocked in British shops and on jukeboxes when Bowie was soaking up American R&B as a kid. During the *Serious Moonlight Tour* in 1983, Bowie would sing a brief snippet from 'Lavender Blue', leading straight into '"Heroes"' in a quietly stunning move.

Rimbaud's *Royauté* may have left another trace. It tells of a man and a woman who, if only for a brief moment, elevate their love to a form of royalty, a fleeting triumph, laughing and trembling in the face of a hostile world. 'I want to be queen!' she cries in the marketplace, a desire that fuses love and power at once. The title could have been sparked by Neu!'s 'Hero', or by *Helden*, a series of ironic paintings dating from 1965 and 1966 by German neo-expressionist Georg Baselitz, steeped in the psychological, moral and cultural fallout of a defeated and divided Germany. These works juxtapose the hollow aesthetics of heroism and propaganda with the vulnerability of the individual, turning triumphalist postures into bleeding, fractured figures of tragicomedy.

Returning to the image of lovers by the Wall: Bowie was drawn to an Otto Mueller painting he encountered at the Brücke-Museum, *Liebespaar Zwischen Gartenmauern*, painted in 1916. It depicts a couple kissing, little more than silhouettes against garden walls overgrown with foliage, reaching for tenderness in a fleeting moment of shared isolation. Painted during Mueller's time as a soldier in the Great War, his choice to depict a secluded kiss within a walled enclosure echoes his deeply personal expressionist ethos: not explosive gestures or bold contrasts, but softness, shelter, intimacy. The kiss lingers, like a shadow: not quite a story, not yet a memory.

Armed with a few sheets of scribbled ideas, Bowie stepped up to the microphone. By then, the 24-track tape was already packed with instrumentation, leaving only one channel for the lead vocal. The handwritten lyric sheets for '"Heroes"' reveal not just finished lines but also blank spaces, stray words and crossings-out, points where the text was still in motion. Listening back through headphones, he built the vocal line by line, instinctively reacting to the track. Visconti would rewind to the last line and punch in the next. The process was swift and cumulative.

To capture the vocal, Visconti devised one of the most celebrated techniques of his career: a set-up of three microphones placed at increasing distances within the vast Meistersaal, designed to capture the room's reverb live. One sat just 20 centimetres from Bowie, another around six metres away and the third was stationed 15 metres across the hall. The two furthest microphones were fitted with electronic gates, set to activate only when Bowie's voice passed a certain volume threshold. In practice, this meant the song's sonic environment expanded as his performance intensified: a quiet murmur would trigger only the close mic, but as he raised his voice, the second mic would open up the room, and eventually the third would flood the take with the full ambient resonance of the hall. Visconti told *Sound On Sound* in 2004:

> The whole idea worked, and what you hear on the record is probably take three. We wouldn't go beyond that. He was really worked up by then, and I can tell you he was feeling it. It was quite an emotional song for him to sing; he deliberated long and hard over these lyrics, and he was ready to go. There was no holding him back.

The set-up spurred Bowie to perform not just with volume, but with emotional escalation, turning a quiet promise into something monumental. The bloom of his voice across the room traces the arc of the song itself: from private moment to public cry, from whispered vow to desperate declaration.

Immediately after the lead vocal was recorded, Bowie asked to add backing vocals. He and Visconti completed two tracks of harmonies, wrapping the entire vocal session in just under five hours, covering lyrics, lead and backing. This is where another ambiguity resurfaces: although more often claimed than actually heard, an uncredited Maass is said to appear on the backing vocals. Assistant engineer Peter Burgon later stated he sang the backing parts with Bowie while Visconti remained in the control room. When engineer Meyer was on holiday in the Caribbean that summer, Burgon had stepped in as engineer, as confirmed by Meyer. Whether the voices on the backing track sound German, British, or Brooklyn is an accentology quest perhaps few would care to pursue. There is richer ground to cover.

Revelation

'And you, you can be mean', Bowie sings with something between a sigh and a subdued chuckle. It hovers somewhere between a tease, a truth and a trace of resignation, followed by 'And I, I'll drink all the time'. In the *Bowie In Berlin* documentary, Shenstone recalls how Bowie would often call her 'mean', usually, she says, after she told him off for drinking and smoking.

That moment anchors a brief second stanza in the song where affection and dysfunction are stated plainly, without fanfare. She can be cutting, he's on the drink and they are lovers: that is a fact – and nothing more. There's no attempt to elevate their connection beyond what it is. If anything, it's the sound of two people who know each other's limits and lean into them regardless. It lends a different shade to the song's opening lines: 'I, I will be king/And you, you will be queen'. They now read less as romantic ideals than as private titles in a crumbling domain, part of a quiet roleplay between lovers, not born of grandeur but of need. 'Though nothing will keep us together' lays their fate bare, while 'We could steal time just for one day' casts it as a furtive grab at freedom.

The vocal phrasing here matters. The doubled pronouns – 'I, I'll', 'you, you will' – give the lines a vulnerable weight, as if each word has to cross a threshold before it can land. The repetition slows the statement, hesitates slightly, and in doing so, intensifies it. It suggests a voice calling itself into being before reaching for the other, a fragile assertion of 'us' made word by word.

'I, I wish you could swim/Like the dolphins, like dolphins can swim' brings a soft, wistful note. It's the first time a line opens with longing. The dolphin isn't symbolic so much as a projection: grace, trust, or simply the ability to move freely in a shared element. The wish suggests the opposite: that the person he's addressing can't. She stays guarded or simply apart. Whatever ease the dolphins represent, it's out of reach.

Then Bowie intensifies, throwing himself into the recurring line – 'I, I will be king' – reclaiming their royalty with a surge of desperation and force. It's a moment that still chills the spine. Now in full: 'We can be heroes, just for one day'. Still carrying irony, not cynicism, flickering on the edge of belief. The tension crackles in the way Bowie hisses 'usss' in 'We can be us', as if forcing it out. Who is 'us' anyway? The couple in a claimed togetherness, in a bare affirmation of being, or in the shared fantasy of who the protagonist promises they could become? Or perhaps it is just an assertion that risks collapsing the moment it is made. The lovers may only exist as truly themselves for a single day, as if their shared identity finds its starkest shape only under exceptional pressure.

It carries an echo of Jean-Paul Sartre's *Being And Nothingness*, where authenticity appears only as a hard-won possibility. Albert Camus' *The Stranger*, listed among Bowie's favourite books, shows how meaning can arise in a sudden act of lucidity. Facing execution, Meursault's final gesture is not hope, but a refusal to lie. A rebellion within the absurd: not escape, but presence. In the end, his act becomes his meaning, just as 'We can be us' becomes its own kind of truth: momentary, defiant and enough.

With 'I can remember', the haze lifts. For the first time, we are placed somewhere: standing by the Wall, under threat, in a moment that cuts through the drift. The kiss – 'We kissed as though nothing could fall' – carries a defiant stillness: not 'and nothing could fall', but a phrase that concedes the inevitability of collapse, while 'fall' carries a historical weight, where walls, lovers and empires tumble. The subjunctive phrasing casts a fleeting illusion, holding catastrophe at bay for the length of a kiss. In Bowie's original draft, the line read 'And the mirror cowered lest we fall', a more self-conscious, metaphorical image, already fearful of failure or exposure. By replacing it with something more immediate, he stepped out of the reflection and let the ambiguity breathe.

The kiss evokes an image held up against erasure, trembling with the effort of staying whole. There's a kinship with Rainer Rilke's *Duino Elegies*, where physical touch strains toward the timeless, and even a fleeting caress may reach across the centuries. Strikingly, the 2019 film *Jojo Rabbit* ends with a passage from *Go To The Limits Of Your Longing* by Rilke, who died in 1926 at the Valmont sanatorium, less than five kilometres from Bowie's house in Blonay, Switzerland. The lines 'Let everything happen to you. Beauty and terror. Just keep going. No feeling is final' are poignantly underscored by '"Helden"', the German version of '"Heroes"'.

In Bowie's lines, love no longer floats above reality; it collides with it. 'And the shame, was on the other side' draws its charge from a city cut and contained. In official East German terms, the Wall was an *antifaschistischer Schutzwall*, a protective barrier against Western fascism. West Berliners, by contrast, called it the *Schandmauer*, the wall of shame. In that context, Bowie's lyric lands as a quiet moral judgement. But it also reflects a deeper irony. The phrase might just as well be repeating the GDR's own narrative, in which East Germany had faced down its fascist past while the Federal Republic proved strikingly pragmatic, letting senior Nazis slip quietly abroad to South America, or into high-level positions in the West. Read that way, the eight words take on added force, turning both propaganda lines back on themselves. It leaves the lovers in the song as witnesses, not victors.

'Maybe we're lying/Then you better not stay', Bowie sings in lucid doubt. The very idea of love against the world, of 'winning', of 'us', may itself be an illusion. It is as if he addresses both the other and himself, a late reflection that questions the utopia, sensing that their defiance may be fragile, even false, yet still real in its intensity. The line sharpens the doubt that had been there all along. They choose to be together – to be us – in a world that denies it. And it is this fleeting, unauthorised, perhaps even forbidden interval that the quotation marks around '"Heroes"' expose: a title that questions itself. The song ends not in glory but in something subtler: an embraced uncertainty. There is no escape, but there is a moment.

Bowie's austere, carefully weighted lines resist closure. Rich with implication, they allow for other readings, each tracing a different fissure in the Wall. In *Melody Maker* in 1977, he described the song as being 'about facing that kind of reality and standing up to it', referring to the atmosphere of isolation and impermanence he had encountered in Berlin. 'The only heroic act one can fucking well pull out of the bag in a situation like that is to get on with life from the very simple pleasure of remaining alive, despite every attempt being made to kill you.' This remark, the evocative idea of 'Bowie in Berlin', the anecdotes of a kiss by the Wall, the possible reference to the Schandmauer and the album credits listing 'Hansa by the Wall' as the recording location have led to a widely shared consensus: the song takes place in Berlin. In one interpretation, the couple stand on opposite sides of the Wall, East and West, reflecting the larger standoff. In that reading, Bowie transforms a fleeting private moment into a symbol of Cold War defiance, breaking through the emotional deadlock of his surroundings with a surge of Romantic idealism. Yet the lyrics remain open, raising questions: is the wall literal or symbolic? Did the kiss happen, or is it imagined?

Like *Liebespaar Zwischen Gartenmauern*, the song evokes classical motifs: forbidden love, hidden meetings. But it goes further, staging a clash between longing and constraint, with fate already closing in. This dramatic arc echoes the tale of Pyramus and Thisbē in Ovid's *Metamorphoses*, later mirrored in *Romeo And Juliet* and *West Side Story*, where lovers are parted by opposing families and speak through a barrier that divides them. Now pull the lovers away from Berlin. Their wall is no longer concrete, no longer patrolled by guards. It is a timeless divider, at once stage-set and legend. Like Pyramus and Thisbē whispering through the cracks, or Juliet behind her balcony, the couple reach for each other across a boundary that both separates and sanctifies their desire. A private myth, held in a suspended moment.

Perhaps he drinks, and she turns cruel, only because they are denied each other by 'them'. But their love is real, and that is that. Perhaps a past meeting ended in gunfire, shame detonated between families that saw love as betrayal. That their story may end in death, like Pyramus and Juliet, makes their desire to steal time all the more piercing. They may not survive, but they can believe, for a moment, that they are safer.

Another reading sets aside the historical backdrop and the borrowed myths. The wall is no border, no *Schandmauer*, no garden wall from an ancient tale, but a rift between two people. The couple are not defiant figures in a torn city, nor players in a story of forbidden love, but fading lovers, caught in the dying flicker of something already broken. She is cruel, he drinks and the 'them' they try to beat are their own habits, their history, their drift apart. 'Though nothing will keep us together' is no prophecy, but a line already lived. Still, he remembers a moment when things felt real, when they kissed as though nothing could fall. If that memory still burns, maybe they can steal time, pretend and delay the end.

In all its forms, '"Heroes"' is a hymn of longing pitched against the madness that walls everything in. Its universal power lies in how it holds fragility and defiance in the same breath, making a single instant feel as if it could outlast time. That ambivalence is what gives '"Heroes"' its force as a soundtrack to both despair and exaltation.

Exodus

After 'Rebel Rebel', '"Heroes"' would become Bowie's most frequently covered song, adopted across genres and generations. It also evolved into one of his most enduring live staples: by the end of his touring life, only 'Fame', 'The Jean Genie' and 'Rebel Rebel' had been played more. Speaking to *Q* in 1990, he acknowledged:

> Recording something in a studio and then putting it in front of a live audience, it becomes a different animal. And it certainly did, that one particularly; I hadn't anticipated the way it would become that kind of anthemic thing.

All the more striking, then, is that the song peaked only at number 24 on the UK Singles Chart when released as a single on 23 September 1977, three weeks before the album's release. Backed with 'V-2 Schneider', it failed to chart at all on the US *Billboard* Hot 100 or the Canadian top 100, although it did reach the top ten and top 20 in several European countries and in Australia. The single was an edited version that reduced the running time from 6:07 to 3:32 and omitted the first two and final verses. As mentioned, it is a cut best consigned to the drawer of denial and strategic amnesia, along with the inconvenient truth that it has since become a mainstay of Bowie compilations.

As compromised as the single version was, it still drew considerable praise at the time. Reception in the UK music press was largely positive, with *Record Mirror* calling it 'regal' and 'shocking, dreamingly powerful', and *ZigZag* describing its climax as 'magic'. *NME* remained grudging in its praise, calling it 'ponderous', while sniping that its 'heavy riff may just be hypnotic enough to drag people into buying it. I hope not.' Still, the magazine placed it at number six in their list of the year's best singles. In the US, *Crawdaddy* hailed it as Bowie's 'best commitment to plastic in three years', the *LA Times* singled out its 'compassion and some fleeting hope', while *Billboard* named it one of the album's standout tracks. The prevailing critical view placed it as a natural fit within Bowie's canon.

Bowie seemed intent on reinforcing that view. He gave it a strong promotional push. A stark video, directed by Stanley Dorfman, showed him in a darkened room, silhouetted against a white backlight and wearing the same leather jacket as on the album cover. He performed the song on several television programmes: *Top Of The Pops*, for which he recorded a separate version with Ricky Gardiner replacing Robert Fripp; Marc Bolan's *Marc*; and, most improbably, Bing Crosby's Christmas special *Merrie Olde Christmas*, filmed just two days after the Bolan taping and scheduled for broadcast on Christmas Eve 1977. Between the taping of *Marc* and its airing several weeks later, Bolan was killed in a car crash. One month on, Crosby also died, prompting Bowie to quip in a 1993 *Q* interview that he had become wary of his television partners at the time.

He also cut French and German-language versions: '"Héros"' and '"Helden"'. The French lyrics were translated by Coco, while the German rendition, a spur-of-the-moment idea from Visconti, was translated in haste and with shaky grammar by his then-girlfriend Maass. Coached line by line, Bowie sings it with conviction. The result is emotionally piercing and a fitting echo of the Berlin landscape in which the album took shape. For the German and French album releases, these alternate vocals were edited into the full-length track, following the opening verses in English.

Its real afterlife, though, would unfold in the years to come. Later honours are too numerous to list, but suffice it to say that a song which long lingered as a semi-marginal Bowie artefact, until Live Aid gave it a new public force, would, over time, rise to near-universal acclaim. In 1999, *Q* listed '"Heroes"' among the 100 greatest singles of all time, as voted by its readers. In 2001, *Uncut* ranked it the 16th best single of the post-punk era. *Rolling Stone* placed the track at number 46 in its 2004 list of the 500 Greatest Songs of All Time before elevating it to 23 in the 2021 revision, while *Time* magazine selected it for its All-Time 100 Songs. *Uncut* named it Bowie's greatest song, whereas Consequence of Sound, *Mojo* and Smooth Radio placed it just behind 'Life On Mars?'. AllMusic called '"Heroes"' 'arguably Bowie's finest song and a true classic.'

After Bowie's death, '"Heroes"' became his most-streamed track on Spotify and re-entered charts worldwide, peaking at number 12 in the UK and number 11 on *Billboard*'s Hot Rock & Alternative Songs. It returned to the top ten in several European markets, including number three on *Billboard*'s Euro Digital Song Sales, number eight in Scotland and number nine in France, and also charted in Italy, Germany, Japan and Australia.

It has circulated far beyond its original context, appearing in advertising, major sporting events, video games, film and television. Its presence across these arenas speaks to the song's enduring resonance and the ways it has been repurposed, reframed and reintroduced to new audiences. The range is striking: from *Christiane F.*, in which it captured Berlin's drug-fuelled despair, to *Moulin Rouge!*, woven into a lavish pop medley, and *The Perks Of Being A Wallflower*, marking a moment of teenage transcendence, among many other screen appearances. One of the most powerful came in the 2009 documentary *The Cove*, which exposed the annual dolphin slaughter in Taiji. After learning about the film, Bowie asked RCA Records to license '"Heroes"' for just $3,000, a fraction of the usual commercial film rate.

Artists who have covered the song on stage or in the studio include Oasis, The Smashing Pumpkins, Travis, Arcade Fire, Blondie, Nico, Moby, Depeche Mode, The Wallflowers, The Magnetic Fields, Motörhead, David Hasselhoff, the 2010 X Factor finalists, Coldplay, Hollywood Vampires, David Byrne, Lady Gaga, Yungblud, Prince and Romy Haag. Aphex Twin reworked Philip Glass' orchestral version by adding Bowie's original vocals. LCD Soundsystem not only performed it live, but also based their song 'All I Want' directly on '"Heroes"', describing it as a tribute. Ted Leo recorded an optimistic version of the song for *Let All The Children Boogie*, a 2010 Bowie tribute album created to support LGBTQ+ youth through the It Gets Better Project. For the 2009 benefit album *War Child Presents Heroes*, Bowie was asked to select a younger act to cover one of his signature songs. He chose TV On The Radio, who responded with a kinetic version of '"Heroes"': equal parts homage and deconstruction. Their cover gained new traction in 2015 when it underscored the trailer for season five of *Game Of Thrones*. A year later, Peter Gabriel's version was used in the first season of *Stranger Things* and reprised in the season three finale. In 2025, the song resurfaced in a new version by Alison Goldfrapp and Lorne Balfe, released as part of the soundtrack to the *Doctor Who* spin-off *The War Between The Land And The Sea*. In 2026, Bowie's original played over the illustrated end-credits sequence of the final episode of *Stranger Things,* sending it back into the UK charts at number 34.

Even in Bowie's own work, faint traces of '"Heroes"' echo both backward and forward. In 'Quicksand', the line 'Just a mortal with potential of a superman' resonates with the ambiguous heroism of the embattled couple, whose all-too-human selves reach beyond their limits, however tenuously. Another song from *Hunky Dory*, 'The Bewlay Brothers', offers its own distant reflections in 'Kings of Oblivion' and 'Just for the day'. So, too, does 'Win' from *Young Americans,* with its bitter aside 'Life lies dumb on its heroes'. Stray flickers reappear in later decades: in the title 'Zeroes', in the 'no hope heroes' of 'Shining Star (Makin' My Love)', and in 'Real Cool World', where he questions 'saintlike and fantastic heroes'. These echoes also surface where wishing meets water: 'Wish I were a sailor/Crossing an azure sea' in 'Run', and 'I wish I was smarter/I got so lost on the shore' in 'Afraid'.

During the 2002 *Heathen Tour,* Bowie placed '"Heroes"' directly before 'Heathen (The Rays)', a pairing whose resonance feels intentional. Where '"Heroes"' frames love as a defiant act of unity in the face of adversity, 'Heathen' circles a similar fragility from a quieter distance, its steel skylines and dying light replacing the Wall with a more internal, post-millennial barricade. Like '"Heroes"', it carries an acute sense of impermanence: 'All things must pass' signals the fading of what once seemed beyond the reach of time. In '"Heroes"', the ambiguous 'them' stands in the way, a presence to be faced head-on through sheer will and mutual resolve. As 'Heathen' unfolds, that opposition becomes the inevitability of mortality, a truth that cannot be defeated but must be endured. Not escaped, but seen clearly, in the Camusian sense of lucidity without consolation. The title speaks to that outlook directly: a world beyond belief, where no higher promise softens the facts of impermanence. It cuts the air when Bowie sings: 'I can see it now, I can feel it die'. 'Looking for someone' and the direct address 'You say you'll leave me' place human connection against that unyielding truth, echoing the way love or passion in '"Heroes"' becomes the vital force that makes it possible to 'win' just for one day. The one day whose sunset falls in 'Heathen', its lovers and the voice that carried them reaching into twilight.

Although Bowie initially hesitated to include '"Heroes"' in the 2015 musical *Lazarus*, wary that it might feel too showbizzy, he changed his mind after hearing its hushed, stripped-back arrangement. The song ultimately served as the closing number in the production, a surreal sequel to *The Man Who Fell To Earth*. Speaking to *Het Parool* in 2019, director Ivo van Hove noted: 'Despite the darkness in *Lazarus*, the final number, '"Heroes"', provides a happy ending. There is hope, we grant each other something and all ordinary people are heroes.'

Bowie attended the show's premiere in Manhattan on 7 December 2015. After the last notes of '"Heroes"' faded, featuring the altered line 'Yes, we're free now/And that is that', he appeared onstage alongside the cast. It turned out to be his last public appearance. The *Lazarus* cast album was recorded at Avatar Studios in New York City on 11 January 2016, the day after Bowie's death. Arriving at the studio unaware, the cast and musicians were met with the news, and their performances that day bear the weight of that moment.

Two years after his passing, the song lingered in the work of his son, now Duncan Jones, whose 2018 film *Mute* opens with Glass' version and echoes the song's motifs in Leo and Naadirah's story, from its recurring dolphins to its future Berlin setting. Alongside inspiration from German expressionist works like *Metropolis* and *M*, composer Clint Mansell cited the Berlin trilogy as a major influence on the film's evocation of Berlin culture.

The song is intertwined with the city's history. In June 1987, shortly before Reagan gave his famous 'Mr. Gorbachev, tear down this wall!' speech at the Brandenburg Gate, the *Glass Spider Tour* reached West Berlin. In the days before the performance, Bowie returned to Hansa Studio for a closed-door session with the band, running through 'Time Will Crawl' as part of a booking arranged to meet a union requirement that his crew be employed at least once that week. He then played a concert near the Wall, as part of the three-day Concert for Berlin festival on the Platz der Republik. The stage stood in front of the Reichstag, once the proud seat of a unified Germany, now a crumbling monument in the shadow of division. The Wall and the Brandenburg Gate loomed nearby, and the sound of the show carried clearly into East Berlin. Thousands of East Berliners gathered on the other side, as close to the Wall as they dared. Rock music was viewed as a destabilising force, and Bowie fans in the East were officially barred from attending, but thanks to Bowie's crew, who pointed the speakers eastward, they could still hear the entire concert. Midway through the set, Bowie turned to the East and said in German: 'We send our wishes to all our friends who are on the other side of the Wall', then launched into an impassioned performance of '"Heroes"'. Recalling the memorable evening in a 2003 interview with *Performing Songwriter*, he said:

> It was one of the most emotional performances I've ever done. I was in tears. They'd backed up the stage to the Wall itself so that the Wall was acting as our backdrop. We kind of heard that a few of the East Berliners might actually get the chance to hear the thing, but we didn't realise in what numbers they would. And there were thousands on the other side that had come close to the Wall. So it was like a double concert where the Wall was the division. And we would hear them cheering and singing along from the other side. God, even now I get choked up. It was breaking my heart. I'd never done anything like that in my life, and I guess I never will again.

As the sound carried over the Wall, border guards moved in and pushed the crowd back, sometimes violently. East Berliners erupted into chants of 'The Wall must fall!' and 'Gorby, get us out!' Bowie had headlined the first evening, and many believed that his performance helped draw an even larger crowd to the Wall over the following nights, when police responded with batons. The crackdown backfired: many eyewitnesses later said it marked a turning point in popular sentiment against the regime. Two years later, the Wall came down. When Bowie died, the German government publicly thanked him with a message that read: 'Goodbye, David Bowie. You are now among Heroes. Thank you for helping to bring down the Wall.'

Through our wider circuit of creative interrelations, we could circle from Berlin back to mime: by 1977, Eno had already made two experimental albums with Fripp before the guitarist added his searing parts to '"Heroes"'.

Above: Bowie, Visconti and Hansa engineer Edu Meyer in the control room of Hansa Studios, 1976. (*Barbara Meyer*)

Right: Promoting *Low* in Paris, June 1977, just ahead of the *"Heroes"* sessions. (*Jean-Claude Deutsch*)

Left: Hansa Studios seen from the Berlin Wall, late 1970s. (*Hansa Studios Archive*)

Right: Death strip at the Wall, with guard tower and Czech hedgehog barrier, August 1977. (*George Louis, CC BY-SA 3.0*)

Left: Potsdamer Platz, November 1975, with graffiti protesting state violence. (*Edward Valachovic, CC BY-SA 2.0*)

Right: Bowie at Hansa Studios during the *"Heroes"* sessions, summer 1977. (*Corinne Schwab*)

Left: The briefcase EMS Synthi AKS, used by Eno to process Fripp's guitar and add electronic textures. (*Soundgas Tech Ltd*)

Right. 'Use an unacceptable colour', a card from Eno's *Oblique Strategies* deck. (*Enoshop*)

Left: Chris Burden performing *Trans-Fixed*, 1972, in a scene from *Burden*. (*Magnolia Pictures*)

Right: 'Sons Of The Silent Age' hints at the shadow of *Fahrenheit 451*'s dystopia. (*Ballantine Books*)

Left: *Head Of Mishima*, painted by Bowie, part of the Hauptstraße apartment interior. (*The David Bowie Archive*)

Right: 'You must see the movie' – a theatrical poster for *Lawrence Of Arabia*, 1963. (*Columbia Pictures*)

Left: *The Secret Lives Of Lawrence Of Arabia*, 1969. (*McGraw-Hill*)

Right: 'The Secret Life Of Arabia' drifts through the mirage world once conjured by *The Desert Song*, 1929. (*Warner Bros*)

Left: The Berlin triptych begins: *New Music: Night And Day* becomes *Low* in 1977. (*RCA/Parlophone/Warner/Jones-Tintoretto*)

Right: The stark, stylised *"Heroes"* sleeve by Masayoshi Sukita, 1977. (*RCA/Parlophone/Warner/Jones-Tintoretto*)

Left: Bowie on the metal support used for *Lodger*'s falling figure, 1979. (*RCA/Parlophone/Warner/Jones-Tintoretto*)

Right: The *Isolar II Tour*, or *Stage Tour*, captured on the 1978 double live album. (*RCA/Parlophone/Warner/Jones-Tintoretto*)

Left: Bowie's narration earned a Grammy nomination for Best Children's Album in 1979. (*RCA/Parlophone/Warner/Jones-Tintoretto*)

Right: The *"Heroes"* cover hijacked for *The Next Day* in 2013: a bold conceptual move. (*ISO/Columbia Records/Jones-Tintoretto*)

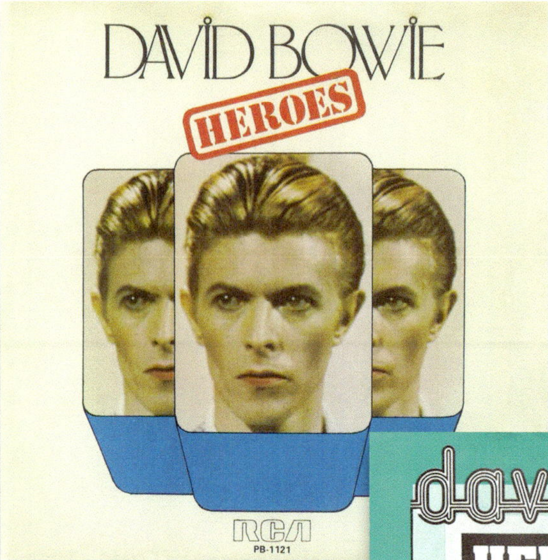

Left: '"Heroes"', backed with 'V-2 Schneider', 7" vinyl single, released in Spain, 1977. (*RCA Victor/Licensed*)

Right: Belgian 7" edition with alternate artwork, 1977. (*RCA Victor/Licensed*)

Left: Bowie appears unconvinced by the sleeve choice on this French-language 7" single, 1977. (*RCA Victor/Licensed*)

Right: German 7” pressing of ‘“Helden”’, crediting Antonia Maass as co-writer, 1977. (*RCA Victor/Licensed*)

Left: ‘Under Japanese influence’ on this 7” single release, 1978. (*RCA Victor/Licensed*)

Right: Multilingual 12” reissue, Germany, 1982. (*RCA Victor/Licensed*)

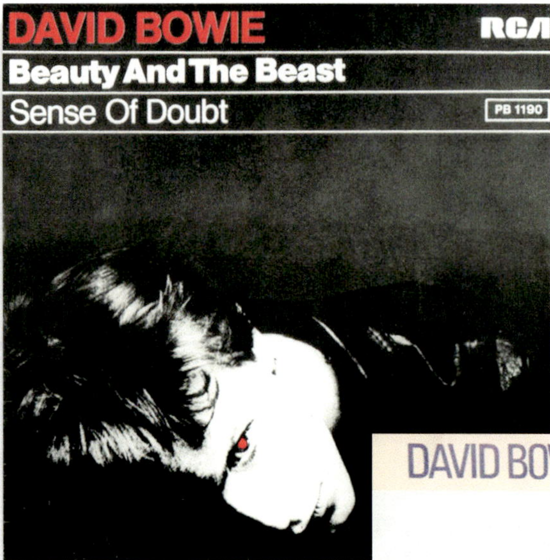

Left: Dutch 7" release of the second single from *"Heroes"*, 1978. (*RCA Victor/Licensed*)

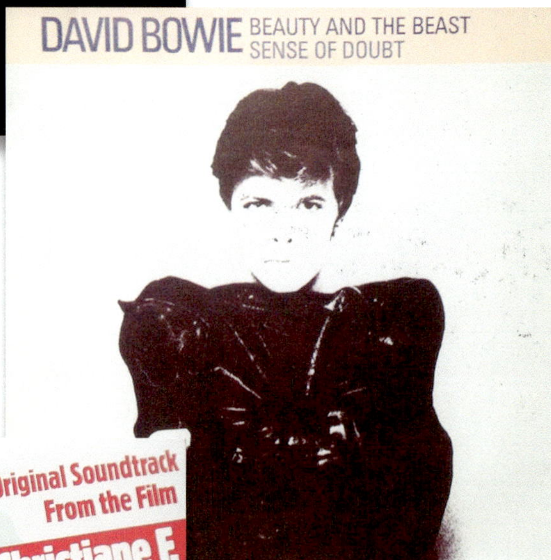

Right: Irish pressing of the 'Beauty And The Beast' 7" single, 1983. (*RCA Victor/Licensed*)

Left: *Christiane F.* soundtrack, built around Bowie's Berlin-era recordings. US release, 1982. (*RCA/Parlophone/Warner/ Jones-Tintoretto*)

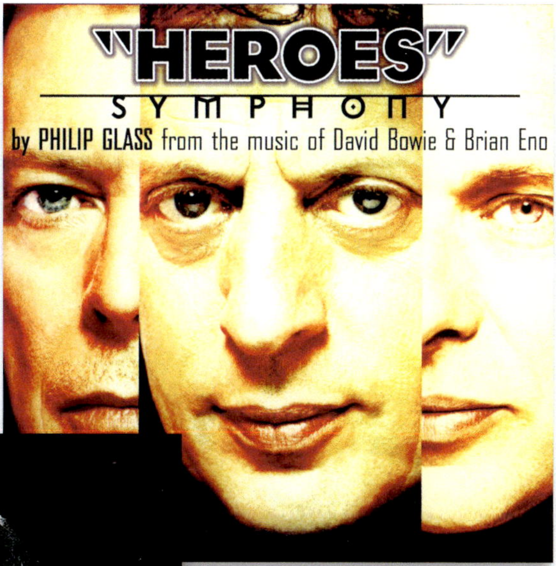

Right: *"Heroes" Symphony* by Philip Glass, with Bowie, Glass and Eno on the cover. UK CD release, 1997. (*Point Music*)

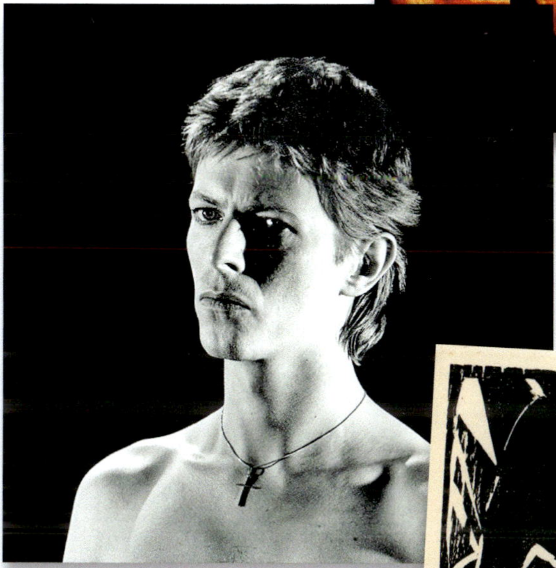

Left: Offstage at Bing Crosby's *Merrie Olde Christmas*, Elstree Studios, September 1977. (*ATV Network, archival PR*)

Right: Though Heckel's better-known painting is usually cited, his *Roquairol* woodcuts suggest a kinship with the *"Heroes"* cover. (*The Met;ARS;VG Bild-Kunst*)

Left: Kirchner's *Bildnis Des Dichters Leonhard Frank*, another motif subtly echoed in the cover's pose. (*PD-Art/PD-US*)

Right: Self-portrait in charcoal, used in promotional material for the 1978 tour. (*The David Bowie Archive/RCA*)

Left: Onstage at the Providence Civic Centre, Rhode Island, May 1978, during the *Stage Tour*. (*Arthur D'Amario III*)

Right and below: Boston Garden, May 1978. Songs from *Ziggy*, *Low* and *"Heroes"* featured prominently in the setlist. (*Arthur D'Amario III*)

Left: 'Lavender blue, dilly, dilly'. As on the *Stage Tour*, '"Heroes"' occupied the second slot in the setlist of the 1983 *Serious Moonlight Tour*. (*Arthur D'Amario III*)

Right: During the 1987 *Glass Spider Tour*, in the year he gave a famously emotional performance of '"Heroes"' in Berlin. (*Arthur D'Amario III*)

Right: *Sound+Vision Tour*, 1990. In the *LA Times*, Bowie called '"Heroes"' 'a song of hope, quite definitely, and me trying to feel hopeful in my own life.' (*Les ZG, CC BY 4.0*)

Below: 'It's a bitch to sing, it's a good one to belt out and I get a kick out of it every time', Bowie told *Q* on the *Reality Tour*. (*Roger Woolman, CC BY 3.0*)

Above: Hauptstraße 155, first floor, Schöneberg, where Bowie and Iggy once lived, photographed in 2026. (*Hans Meertens*)

Below: A plaque honouring Bowie, unveiled in August 2016 at his former apartment. (*OTFW, CC BY-SA 3.0*)

Fripp would later join bassist Tony Levin in the reincarnated King Crimson, by which time Levin had already become a mainstay in Peter Gabriel's band. Gabriel had brought in Fripp on his debut, collaborated with Eno on his second and both he and King Crimson would later cover '"Heroes"'. In the early 2000s, the song became a fixture of King Crimson's live shows, with both Fripp and Adrian Belew on stage. Belew had first played it alongside Bowie on the 1978 *Stage Tour*, and was Bowie's guitarist on *Lodger* as well as during the *Sound+Vision Tour* in 1990. That same year, he dueted with Bowie on 'Pretty Pink Rose', and Bowie supplied lyrics and vocals for his track 'Gunman'. Belew also played on Talking Heads' *Remain In Light*, which Eno produced, and on Gabriel's 'Out Out', helmed by Nile Rodgers, who later produced *Let's Dance,* 'Real Cool World' and *Black Tie White Noise*. In her 1982 video for 'The Dreaming', long-time Bowie admirer Kate Bush appeared in a spacesuit identical to the one Bowie had worn in 'Ashes To Ashes'. In 1987, a rare split single paired a track by Eno with one by Bush, who by then had duetted with Gabriel on 'Don't Give Up', with Tony Levin on bass, as he would be on 'Where Are We Now?', Bowie's late, elliptical return to the ghost-traced streets of Berlin. The signal, always humming, finds its way to an early silhouette: both Bush and Gabriel had studied under Lindsay Kemp, whose mime classes had once drawn in a shy, self-reinventing young man at the beginning of his career.

'Sons Of The Silent Age'

The weighty task of following the album's thunderous centrepiece fell to its sole pre-written song: a majestic, futuristic dreamscene, coloured by Bowie's twilight-hued, elegiac saxophone lines. 'He played with Art Pepper elegance', Visconti later wrote in *A New Career In A New Town*, though a 1979 *New York Rocker* review dismissed his saxophone on 'Sons Of The Silent Age' as 'tacky and inadequate'.

Bowie's sax playing has long divided opinion, attracting both admiration and scepticism. He himself was under no illusions about his limitations: 'I really have to go through traumas to get anything out of it that has anything to do with what I want it to say. So it's not a steady relationship; it's not a good one', he told *Musician* in 1983. What some heard as imperfection, others recognised as bold artistic instinct. Nile Rodgers told *Rolling Stone* in 1993. 'I think David would be the first to admit he is not a saxophonist in the traditional sense. He uses his playing as an artistic tool. He's a painter. He hears an idea, and he goes with it. But he absolutely knows where he's going.' That perspective resonates with what *Blackstar* keyboardist Jason Lindner told *JazzTimes* in 2024: Bowie 'probably doesn't have chops or versatility, but he uses the instrument in a sonic way and in an emotional, expressive way.' In Bowie's work, the saxophone was always more than an instrument: a vessel for inner states and otherness, nourished by early memories and influences.

Ten years his senior, Bowie's half-brother Terry had introduced the young David to science fiction, Buddhism, Beat poetry and modern jazz: Mingus, MJQ, Coltrane, Dolphy, Coleman. In the stolid sprawl of Bromley, where Bowie spent much of his childhood, those sounds and ideas pointed beyond the suburb's limits and would continue to infuse his body of work. Terry suffered from severe mental illness and was eventually institutionalised, a fate that left a deep imprint on Bowie and would continue to haunt his lyrics for decades.

As these artistic seeds were being planted, Bowie began his lifelong connection to the saxophone. At 14, David received his first – a fragile white Grafton – from his father for Christmas, but it lacked projection and broke easily. The acrylic instrument was the only item he later refused to loan for the *David Bowie Is* exhibit, as it held special significance for him. Soon after receiving it, he persuaded his father to buy him a better model, bought on hire purchase. The replacement, a Conn tenor, was used during his time with his first band, The Konrads, and he played it on his first single, 'Liza Jane', released in 1964 and credited to Davie Jones with the King Bees. The same sax appeared on the back cover of his 1973 album *Pin Ups*. Throughout his later career, Bowie would collaborate with several jazz luminaries, including Pat Metheny, Lester Bowie, Cuong Vu, Maria Schneider and Donny McCaslin.

While Terry exposed him to modern jazz, it was the energy of early rock 'n' roll that lit the spark. In a 2003 interview with *Performing Songwriter*, Bowie recalled how the saxophone captured his imagination:

> When I was nine and first saw Little Richard in a film that played around town – I think it was probably *Girl Can't Help It* – seeing those four saxophonists onstage, it was like, 'I want to be in that band!' And for a couple of years, that was my ambition: to be in a band playing saxophone behind Little Richard. That's why I got a saxophone.

In the spring of 1962, eager to learn, the young Bowie searched through early copies of *Melody Maker* and discovered that one of the leading saxophonists on the British jazz scene was Ronnie Ross, an acclaimed baritone player. He noted that Ross lived in Abingdon, looked him up in the phone book, and boldly asked for lessons. The first three were weekly, then fortnightly, charged at £2 an hour. The lessons continued for three or four months, until August, when Bowie joined The Konrads. Ross later recalled, as quoted in *Alias David Bowie:*

> He arrived highly motivated and was well prepared for the learning. He was quite shy, but he had a good sense of humour. He definitely showed an aptitude for music, and he was very interested in jazz. You notice when people work at things, because some people, when they come back, give excuses, they've been busy. But he always came back, and he'd done what I'd given him to do. He was a student, and he wanted to learn.

For the rest of his life, Bowie remained attached to the instrument, returning to it time and again in both live and studio settings, from 'Changes', 'Soul Love', 'Sorrow', and 'Sweet Thing' to 'Tiny Girls' from *The Idiot* and 'Subterraneans' from *Low*. As producer of the record, Bowie is often mythically credited with the iconic baritone sax solo on Lou Reed's 'Walk On The Wild Side' from the landmark album *Transformer*. In reality, it was his old sax teacher Ross, whom Bowie personally brought in to play the part on the doo-wop-inspired classic.

Another song heavily influenced by 1950s doo-wop, 'Drive-In Saturday' from *Aladdin Sane* radiates future nostalgia, imagining a post-apocalyptic world where people have forgotten how to make love and rely on old films as instruction manuals. 'Sons Of The Silent Age' closes with a doo-wop tinge and sketches a similarly fragmented vision of a faded future. Further echoes emerge: both 'The Supermen' from *The Man Who Sold The World* and 'Oh! You Pretty Things' from *Hunky Dory* are Nietzschean in scope, the former mythic and gnostic, the latter apocalyptic and evolutionary, while 'Sons Of The Silent Age' suggests spectral, urban suspension. Yet all three depict a generation bordering on the superhuman, trapped in emotional emptiness, estrangement, and fatalism.

Perhaps at heart a bleak Burroughsian cut-up collage of dreamlike fragments wrapped around a melodramatic refrain, 'Sons Of The Silent Age' has, over the years, been read as a portrait of the emotionally sedated commuter, drifting through muted cycles of routine, as a response to the rise of punk in the UK, or even as a reflection of Bowie's own psychic state in the wake of his post-LA detox. Yet it also invites a darker, more historical reading. Could the 'silent age' refer to pre-war Germany, an era of quiet complicity, when spiritual vacancy and silent censorship enabled the destructive rise of authoritarian rule? Bowie had long explored dystopian systems and the psychology of mass control: from the grotesque utopianism of 'We Are Hungry Men' to the mechanised tyranny of 'Saviour Machine', culminating in the Orwellian *Diamond Dogs*. 'Sons Of The Silent Age' fits within that lineage as a psychological portrait of submission. Bowie's sons are not the rulers; they are the ruled. They do not resist but drift. And in drifting, they obey.

As early as 'Cygnet Committee' from 1969, Bowie had already turned against mindless compliance, explicitly criticising the apathy he saw within the counterculture movement. Speaking to *Music Now!* that year, he said:

> 'Cygnet Committee' is one way of using a song. But these people – they're so apathetic, so lethargic. The laziest people I ever met in my life. They don't know what to do with themselves. Looking all the time for people to show them the way. They wear anything they're told, and listen to any music they're told to. People are like that.

The remark resonates when the names Sam Therapy and King Dice appear in 'Sons Of The Silent Age', presented as musical acts. Another echo surfaces: in

1976, during his interview with *Playboy*, while inhabiting his Thin White Duke persona, Bowie provocatively claimed: 'Rock stars are fascists, too. Adolf Hitler was one of the first rock stars', pointing to how the seductive power of the stage could shade into authoritarian control. Drawing on that idea, Sam Therapy and King Dice emerge less as mere characters than as dark emblems in a totalitarian allegory: the silent hand within, and the smiling executioner of chance. Notably, the name Sam would reappear in 'Scream Like A Baby' on *Scary Monsters*, a chilling dystopian vision of incarceration, erasure and psychological control.

Bowie never spells it out, but the emotional and behavioural patterns he describes – repression, inertia, fading away – could just as easily belong to a generation that looked away when it mattered most. In their passivity, detachment and emotional sedation, the sons of the silent age seem to echo what political philosopher Hannah Arendt famously described as 'the banality of evil': not the loud violence of monsters, but the quiet compliance of ordinary people who neither think nor resist. 'They never die, they just go to sleep one day' suggests not only passivity or disappearance, but also the unsettling potential of dormancy, awaiting the right conditions to reawaken. In that sense, Bowie's sons are not merely ghosts of the past, but latent agents of obedience, waiting for history to repeat itself.

Bowie's line recalls Jacques Brel's 'Les Vieux', via its English version in the musical revue *Jacques Brel Is Alive And Well And Living In Paris*. Bowie included the 1968 cast recording in his 2003 *Vanity Fair* list of 25 favourite albums, and had earlier performed versions of 'My Death' and 'Amsterdam' from that same revue. Another Brel song on that album, 'Fils De…' ('Sons Of…'), may even have sparked the song's title, which also evokes the silent film era, perhaps mirroring the emotional stasis of the song's own muted characters. Bowie was a regular at Notausgang, a small arthouse cinema near Hauptstraße, where classic silent films featured prominently, a world he had felt an affinity with for years. 'They don't walk, they just glide in and out of life' also recalls T. S. Eliot's *The Hollow Men* from 1925, with its spectral image of 'shape without form, shade without colour, paralysed force, gesture without motion', a kind of suspended animation, drained of real vitality.

This idea may even extend to the internalised lives of gay men in 1930s Berlin, a city that, despite its vibrant queer nightlife during the Weimar years, offered no real safety. Beneath the surface of cabarets and clubs, most visible in Schöneberg, lay a shadow world of coded encounters and private longing, shaped by criminalisation and social risk. It finds a literary counterpart in Isherwood's Berlin novels, which capture the duality of such lives: fleeting intimacy, social invisibility and a constant negotiation between desire and danger, lived as if gliding in and out of life. 'They pick up in bars and cry only once' and 'Make love only once but dream and dream' suggest this tension, where physical love may be possible, but rarely safe, while the imagination remains restless and unresolved: a way of living more in fantasy than in reality, as is often the fate of the marginalised. In this light, the ecstatic refrain ('Let's find another way in/Sons of sound, and Sons of sound') almost reads as a call to come out of hiding, to escape the silence and claim a life of presence, voice and connection.

Characteristic of the album's lyrics, 'Sons Of The Silent Age' is a quintessential Bowie collage: suggestive, associative and steeped in imaginative ambiguity, offering layers of connotation without imposing a single, linear meaning, only deepening its allure. Tellingly, even a brief phrase like 'no books' carries heavy implications. Within the world of 'Sons Of The Silent Age', it evokes a cultural void: people still moving through the motions, yet with nothing left to draw from. No ideas, no stories, no memory. It strikes at the core of Ray Bradbury's *Fahrenheit 451*: a society where books are outlawed because they dare people to think. Bradbury had already influenced Bowie almost a decade earlier, with *The Illustrated Man* inspiring lines in 'Karma Man' and his short story *Kaleidoscope* echoing in 'Space Oddity'. More recently, imagery from *Something Wicked This Way Comes* had resurfaced in 'Future Legend'. In *Fahrenheit 451*, the citizens have been untrained in feeling and detached from meaning, wearing the same vacant expressions as Bowie's sons, who linger on platforms but seem to be going nowhere. They look, but lack sight ('All I see is all I know'). It's a potent metaphor, as in François Truffaut's 1966 film adaptation of *Fahrenheit 451*, where people seem adrift in a world that no longer remembers why it's moving.

As with so much in the Bowieverse, the threads are dizzyingly interconnected, beginning with the most famous son of the silent film age, Charlie Chaplin, who came from the same corner of South London as Bowie. Truffaut openly admired Chaplin's cinema, calling it a model of simplicity and emotional clarity. His *Fahrenheit 451* featured Nicolas Roeg as cinematographer, who would direct *The Man Who Fell To Earth*. Before Roeg's film, Bowie had drawn on Alice Cooper's shock theatrics while shaping Ziggy Stardust. In a 2021 interview with *Metal Hammer*, Cooper remembered Bowie bringing The Spiders From Mars to one of his shows, telling them, 'This is what we should be doing.' In a 2016 *Rolling Stone* article, Cooper joked about a surreal 1970s dinner with Bowie and Bradbury: 'These guys were in outer space somewhere, they were talking about quantum physics, and I'm going, 'So … what kind of car are you driving?'' Bradbury later reflected on Chaplin's cinematic humanity and satire in the 2002 documentary *The Tramp And The Dictator*. After his Berlin years, Bowie briefly enlisted Chaplin's last wife, Oona O'Neill, to advise on the interior of his Lausanne residence. Charlie and Oona's son Eugene had earlier assisted engineer Dave Richards on the final mixes of *"Heroes"* in Montreux before Bowie became their neighbour as a Swiss resident.

The undercurrents gathered. 'For me,' Michael Caine said in *The Guardian* in 2009, 'the greatest will always be Charlie Chaplin.' Caine, who in 2006 appeared alongside Bowie in *The Prestige*, discovered after his mother's death in 1989 that she had kept a secret from him for 50 years: an elder half-brother, named David, born out of wedlock and institutionalised at Cane Hill Hospital as a teenager. Charlie Chaplin's mother, Hannah, was also institutionalised at Cane Hill, first in 1898 and repeatedly in the years that followed, the same asylum where Bowie's half-brother Terry was later a patient until his tragic death by suicide in 1985. Bowie returned to that dark inheritance in 1993 with 'Jump They Say', a taut, jazz-inflected track on which he played a haunting saxophone himself.

'Blackout'

On the night of 13-14 July 1977, lightning struck a series of substations along the Hudson and in Yonkers, triggering a cascade of failures. Within minutes, New York City went dark. Over the next 25 hours, the blackout unleashed chaos: looting, arson, more than a thousand fires, hundreds injured and a record 3,776 people taken into custody in the largest police operation in city history. More than 6,000 kilometres away, Bowie had just begun recording new material. Given his speed and sensitivity to external events, he likely picked up on the blackout's imagery of breakdown and unrest, whether through AFN broadcasts or osmosis. The frantic intensity and delirious lyrics of 'Blackout' certainly resonate with the images of social and urban collapse that defined that night.

The lyrics veer between disorientation, compulsion and the urge to escape. They open in a feverish tableau: a scalding face, a cage and rotting wine, poisoned intimacy already slipping into sickness. The volatile scene intensifies into a spiralling crisis saturated with panic, obsession and the imminent threat of disintegration.

Bowie's cries of 'Get me to a doctor', 'Get me off the streets' and 'Give me some direction' hit as desperate pleas in a world without footing. Constructed using Burroughs' cut-up technique, the song resists narrative. Set against the band's assault, firepowered by Davis' one-man army frenzy and Bowie's disembodied performance, its very form evokes a disjointed and overwrought condition, teetering on the edge.

The tainted image of 'rotting wine' carries forward a motif of conspicuous drinking, following earlier references to alcohol in 'Joe The Lion' and the title track. 'Virtually every time I saw him in Berlin, he was drunk, or working on getting drunk, and his stress level seemed as high as in his several-grams-a-night period', Angie later recalled in *Backstage Passes*. Doctor, booze, collapse: small wonder, then, that 'Blackout' has often been read as a metaphor for Bowie's physical breakdown in Berlin, after yet another fierce row with Angie in late 1976. He was rushed to the British Army clinic with chest pains and a suspected heart attack, later diagnosed as an anxiety attack triggered by alcohol and exhaustion. Soon after, unsettled by the extent of Coco's control over Bowie's life, Angie stormed into the Schöneberg apartment, threw Coco's clothes out of the window, called a cab and flew to

London, as she described in *Backstage Passes*. This marked the final crack in their marriage. Angie's disruptive stay has also been cited as a possible catalyst for the track's unnerving volatility, particularly in the line 'Someone's back in town/The chips are down'.

Asked by *Uncut* in 1999 whether the song referenced his collapse in Berlin or the New York City power cut of 1977, Bowie replied: 'It did indeed refer to power cuts. I can't, in all honesty, say that it was the New York one, though it is entirely likely that that image locked itself in my head.' He suggested checking both the recording and the New York blackout dates to 'make an intelligent assumption' as to whether he had actually been there. Bowie returned to the subject in a 2003 interview with *The Word*, reflecting on that year's Northeast blackout and the unexpected human closeness it brought. Although he also noted that he had indeed been present during the 1977 power outage, the documented recording schedule for *"Heroes"* makes it highly unlikely he was in New York that night. It seems he was blending memory and influence, much like the track itself. Perhaps even his surroundings: in wartime Berlin, blackouts had been a matter of survival. Windows were sealed with blankets, streetlights extinguished, every glimmer of light a potential target for Allied bombers. By 1977, Bowie was living quite literally among the ruins.

Bombed-out façades, deserted industrial yards, foreign troops and invisible fault lines still shaped the city's surface. 'What if the everyday environment was itself a huge mental breakdown: how could we know if we were sane or psychotic?' This question, posed by one of Bowie's favourite authors, J. G. Ballard, in his 2008 memoir *Miracles Of Life*, lingers over the psychological terrain that the songs on *"Heroes"* seem to inhabit. Ballard, who mused in a 1985 *XS* interview that he'd 'quite like to write the script of a pop video for David Bowie', was himself heavily influenced by Burroughs, and shared Bowie's fascination with fractured perception and unstable realities. On 'Blackout', such imagery unravels in the throes of derailment, a state of overload in which language shatters into rhythmic shards that rain down on the listener. It mirrors 'Beauty And The Beast', drawing on remnants of the same jigsawed patchwork. 'Smile at least' and 'Someone could get skinned' echo 'Your lips cut a smile on your face' and 'Getting some skin exposure', while 'Standing on our feet' and 'Someone fetch a priest' find their counterparts in 'Get me on my feet' and 'Get me to a doctor', each tracing a point along the same neurotic axis of disarray and composure.

In the opening track, beauty is irresistible and potentially destructive; here, that notion returns in the image 'She was a beauty in a cage'. Both cuts suggest that beauty does not liberate but entraps, a motif that recurs throughout the album, where identity falters under pressure and remains suspended between outward roles and private ruptures. There is something elusive and ambiguous in the way Bowie addresses the unnamed 'you' across *"Heroes"*. It often feels just tangible enough to be human, while remaining vague enough to suggest an unstable and shifting force. In 'Blackout', the 'you' remains undefined but serves as a focal point for longing, menace and inner meltdown. It appears to be a lover slipping away – 'You walk on past', 'If you don't stay tonight' – yet trails a heat-haze of unrest: 'Your scalding face', 'your fearful hands'. The other is personified but may just as well be a projection of psychic drift. The 'you' is both intimate and abstract: a lover, a split-off self, a looming danger.

Such slippages in identity run through Bowie's body of work, laced with cultural icons cast in ever-shifting roles: Crowley, Warhol, Guevara, Twiggy, Garbo, Lennon, Dylan, Monroe. Quite a few of these, curiously, also appear as Disney figures, from Beauty, the Beast and Tarzan to Mickey Mouse and the seven dwarfs from *Snow White*. Even Aladdin, if we allow a loose interpretation. As in this track, where the comically defiant 'Me, I'm Robin Hood and I puff on my cigarette' signals a slip into a projected persona, a fictional identity serving as a protective mask against psychological turmoil. A hero on the brink, caught between moral hauteur and inner unravelling. The equally cryptic 'I'm under Japanese influence and my honour's at stake' becomes his report from the edge, where loyalty, pride and self-discipline collide with street-level chaos and theatrical psychosis.

Bowie's delivery slips in and out of sync, stretching phrases like 'I will take that plane tonight' or 'kiss you in the rain' across the barlines, adding to the disorientation that drags against the song's nervous momentum. That energy is fuelled by the band, who sound immense and manic, turning what could have ended up as a straight-ahead rock piece into a hybrid of R&B groove, rock propulsion and early industrial bite. It is the kind of collision that shakes up familiar styles and intercuts them with jarring, destabilising dissonance, enriching the layered, boundary-pushing character of Bowie's music.

Fripp's treated guitar squeals evoke flashing lights, sirens and chaos, while a left-panned Alomar anchors the mix with one of his signature tight, syncopated rhythms. Eno layers in spectral treatments and warbling synths that hover in and out of focus, while Murray's bass plays melodically without ever becoming dominant, sliding seamlessly into the track's unstable sonic landscape. Structurally, the song is built on two underlying frameworks, with Bowie's vocal arranged in three separate sections, each reinforcing the track's disoriented momentum. 'It has the most swagger of any Bowie track', Visconti told TIDAL in 2018. 'We were working with Iggy Pop at the time, and Iggy had a big influence on David in the sense that he was a true punk artist. He did what the hell he wanted. He'd just take his clothes off, randomly. I mean, that guy has swagger!' He reflected:

> David didn't really have that; no matter how outrageous he was, he always had a touch of conservatism about him. One of David's friends at the time said the whole album was very masculine. Too masculine. We disagreed, but we liked that we'd gotten across a different attitude because David's work

> was always more theatrical than masculine. Plus, it wasn't just down and dirty swagger. So you're seeing that coming out of David here, especially, and all over the album. It prevails on the whole album. But 'Blackout' is really the one for me.

The real star here is Dennis Davis, whose drumming drives the entire piece with force and flair. Positioned on a choir riser in the spacious Meistersaal, which could accommodate up to 150 musicians, Davis played live, separated only by isolation panels, or 'gobos'. With his regular kit delayed on its way to the studio, his self-assembled setup included congas and timpani, lending the track an almost orchestral percussive sweep. 'He's a wacko guy, one of the best drummers I've ever worked with', Visconti told *Sound On Sound* in 2004. 'He's not only an innovative drummer but a human metronome, and he's also a jazz guy who never plays the same thing twice.' In the mixing stage, Visconti occasionally modified Davis' sound using the illustrious Harmonizer, with its 'mash drum sound, that depressive, gorilla effect', as Bowie put it in *Musician* in 1983. The natural ambience of the Hansa hall already gave the drums atmosphere and punch, but the Harmonizer added a faint metallic edge and pitch-shifted bite. Less dominant than on *Low*, it still remained an integral colour in the sonic palette. In *A New Career In A New Town*, Visconti recalled:

> For 'Blackout', Dennis found a lonely conga drum in the studio and placed it on one end of his toms rack. Sometimes he played it as part of the rhythm pattern and sometimes as part of a drum fill. Check out the stunning fills at 0:58 and 2:02. By now, he very much approved of the Eventide Harmonizer as part of his sound.

Davis, whose playing here ranks among his most imaginative and infectiously free performances, shared that enthusiasm: 'It sounded like a floor tom with snares on the bottom', he told *Sound International* in 1978. 'That's a really fine thing to do if you are playing some really hard backbeat rock 'n' roll!'

'V-2 Schneider'

By early 1976, Bowie was turning away from the funk and soul lustre of *Young Americans*, 'Golden Years' and 'Stay', and drifting further towards European minimalism, motorik rhythm and ascetic electronics. The signal was unmistakable. On the *Station To Station Tour*, before the band struck a single note, the audience were met with something else entirely: the cool, mechanical drift of Kraftwerk's 'Radioactivity' over the PA, along with scenes from Buñuel and Dalí's surrealist short *Un Chien Andalou*, including the infamous close-up of an eye being sliced open with a razor.

The initial idea had been to get the German electronic pioneers to open the tour, but Kraftwerk declined. This was consistent with their policy of radical self-containment: no collaboration, no cross-pollination, no compromise. Whether their refusal would have remained in place had Bowie not already backed away on practical grounds remains an open question.

Bowie had been drawn to Kraftwerk as early as 1974: his imported copy of *Autobahn* pulled his attention back to Europe, hinting at a future beyond soul stylings and West Coast burnout. Reflecting in *Mojo* in 2002, he said:

> I just got so hooked on this band: Who are they? Who are they connected to? And so I came across Tangerine Dream and CAN and eventually Neu! and this whole new sound happening in Germany. I thought, 'Wow, I've seen the future and it sounds like this.' I very much wanted to be in the swim.

In late 1975, as they explored ideas for the abandoned soundtrack to *The Man Who Fell To Earth*, Bowie and Buckmaster worked from Bowie's Bel Air home, playing *Autobahn* and *Radio-Activity* on repeat. 'We both enjoyed their records very much', Buckmaster recalled in *Kraftwerk: Produktion*. 'We kind of took them seriously, but we kind of laughed as well. Not at it, but because the music had a kind of innocent quality which was very fetching, and a deadpan humour as well.'

Kraftwerk emerged from West Germany's experimental underground in the early 1970s, soon lumped by the British press under the dismissive term Krautrock. Founders Ralf Hütter and Florian Schneider had met in 1968 at the Academy of Arts in Remscheid, bonding over early electronics and Fluxus-inspired aesthetics. They formed Kraftwerk in 1970, set up their Düsseldorf studio Kling Klang, and began recording improvised instrumentals with producer Konrad 'Conny' Plank. Conventional instruments soon gave way to tone generators, hand-built drum machines and self-designed vocoders. High-end synthesisers were beyond their budget, so they built their own. Schneider even held patents for several of the group's custom electronic drum systems. By 1975, with Wolfgang Flür and Karl Bartos on board, Kraftwerk had evolved into a fully self-contained unit. *Autobahn* and *Radio-Activity* introduced their 'robot pop': clean lines, clipped rhythms and a stylised image that evoked machine efficiency in human form. Identical suits, blank expressions and a stage presence like retro-futurist mannequins running on batteries. It was an aesthetic of deliberate construction. In post-war Germany, where nationalism was tainted and cultural identity fraught, Kraftwerk reclaimed a modernist lineage through strict design principles, industrial imagery and the unapologetic use of German.

Over time, the direct influence of Kraftwerk on the sound of *Low* and *"Heroes"* has been overstated. 'Most of it is lazy analyses, I believe', Bowie told *Uncut* in 1999. 'What I was passionate about in relation to Kraftwerk was their singular determination to stand apart from stereotypical American chord sequences and their wholehearted embrace of a European sensibility displayed through their music. This was their very important influence on me.' Where Kraftwerk mapped a direction, Neu! stirred the impulse. His top choice for guitar on *"Heroes"* had been Neu! guitarist Michael Rother, 'Neu! being passionate, even diametrically opposite to Kraftwerk', Bowie pointed out. He had followed the band closely, drawn to a sharp-edged momentum Kraftwerk never quite matched. Rother had attended the same gymnasium as Schneider and had briefly played with Kraftwerk before founding Neu!, also produced by Plank. In 1976, shortly before the *Low* sessions, Bowie visited Plank at his farmhouse near Köln to propose working together on the album. Plank turned him down, citing concerns over Bowie's mental state and drug use. Plans to collaborate with Rother never materialised, either: each mistakenly assumed the other had pulled out, only realising the mix-up decades later.

Bowie met the members of Kraftwerk several times during the *Station To Station Tour*, in Düsseldorf and Frankfurt, and hosted Hütter and Schneider at the end-of-tour party in Paris. They floated the idea of producing each other's albums more than once, more out of courtesy than real intention, as their musical instincts proved too far apart. Bowie, however, felt a genuine affection for them, especially appreciating Schneider's deadpan wit. In Düsseldorf, the two of them toured cake shops, devoured oversized pastries and, at Schneider's insistence and to Bowie's delight, went shopping for asparagus. Kraftwerk immortalised one of these encounters on the title track of *Trans-Europe Express* in 1977: 'From station to station, back to Düsseldorf City, meet Iggy Pop and David Bowie', with a fleeting image of Bowie and Iggy in the original German video. Later that year, Bowie returned the compliment by naming a track after Florian: 'V-2 Schneider'. It was less an imitation than an invocation. Bowie didn't sound like Kraftwerk, but he wanted their ghost in the machine.

Before finding fame, Bowie had played in The Manish Boys and The Lower Third, performing American R&B and soul covers in the mod-inflected style popularised by British bands such as The Spencer Davis Group, The Pretty Things, The Yardbirds and The Animals. These groups belonged to the same circuit that translated American soul and blues into a harder, more propulsive and distinctly local sound. 'V-2 Schneider', the B-side opener, kicks off with a bassline that draws on the same driving, syncopated ostinato heard in The Spencer Davis Group's 'Gimme Some Lovin''. It reflects the shared musical grammar of 1960s London: blues-rooted, repetitive and insistently rhythmic. This bass figure, marked by its signature drop to a lower note, had already surfaced in Bowie's 'Join The Gang', and would later return in 'Strangers When We Meet'. Even the iconic 'Under Pressure' bassline spins the same idea into an unforgettable hook.

Here, over a shrieking whine that evokes a ballistic missile, the bassline is punctuated by insistent snare rolls: a human mimicking the mechanical precision of a machine designed to mimic a human. In combination with the title, the marching fills conjure a sense of militarism – a parade in motion, an echo of the Third Reich, with the V-2 rocket at its centre: a Nazi-manufactured, unmanned weapon designed by Wernher von Braun, who later helped lead the US space programme. Although the song's title was drawn from Schneider's nickname, the association with the rocket remains intact.

For the vocal hook, Bowie and Visconti had intended to use a vocoder, or 'robovox', but none were available. Instead, they programmed four separate synthesiser patches to mimic the vowel sounds of 'Vee-Too-Schnei-Der', while Bowie supplied the consonants live, his voice electronically filtered to remove all body. The use of a vocoder – even a fake one – was pure Kraftwerk. But as if to subvert their robotic rigidity, Bowie leaves a mistake in: his distorted sax enters on the wrong beat, and he runs with it, true to the improvisational spirit of the sessions. In 1999, Bowie told *Uncut* that his aim since *Station To Station* had been 'the hybridisation of R&B and electronics', bringing groove, fluidity and expressive phrasing into dialogue with electronic structure and texture. That tension animates the track: a tight motorik groove offset by a saxophone that stumbles in and never quite settles. 'It's still a very organic, blues-driven sound', Bowie told *Mojo* in 2002, reflecting on the Berlin trilogy. 'If I took what I'd found in America, brought it back to Europe and combined it with what was happening in a sonic way in Germany, I'd just see what would happen.'

'V-2 Schneider' evokes a curious kind of déjà vu: the central melody doesn't recall anything specific, yet it feels instantly familiar. 'Speed Of Life' shares a similar sense of timeless recognition. It stands as a quiet testament to Bowie's ability to embed deceptively simple motifs and hooks in a track without calling attention to the craft or overstating their effect. This instinct for melodic immediacy was something Michael Jackson grasped intuitively, even within a very different musical sphere. Like Bowie, he knew how to carve something memorably new out of minimal, familiar elements, letting it unfold with such clarity that it felt inevitable. Jackson combined this mastery with electronics and machine-tight grooves grounded in Black musical tradition, a sonic terrain Bowie, Eno and the DAM trio had already begun exploring.

Where Jackson's music was rooted in groove and physical instinct, Kraftwerk achieved a comparable effect through restraint and formal control, using repeated figures so refined they seem to hover outside of time. Their melodies rarely unfold in lyrical arcs; instead, they imprint themselves through pure shape and placement. As with Bowie, the sense of déjà vu stems not from reference but from design, motifs so precise they feel discovered rather than invented.

The connection was no mere coincidence. By the mid-1980s, Jackson had become so fascinated by *The Man-Machine* that he approached Hütter and Schneider to request access to the original multitracks, a telling move from an artist obsessed with sonic perfection. True to Kraftwerk's ethos of artistic autonomy, the request was declined. According to Kraftwerk promoter

Maxime Schmitt in *Man, Machine And Music*, Jackson even met Hütter in person at one of his private buildings in New York. As Schmitt recalls, Hütter told him he had been greeted by 'three or four guys', all dressed like Jackson. 'Each time he thought it was Michael Jackson – in fact, they were fakes. A very Kraftwerkian concept', Schmitt remarked.

Besides their love for Kraftwerk, more often than acknowledged and despite their different musical styles, Bowie and Jackson shared much in common. Both mastered the art of self-invention, using masks and characters to amplify their artistic expression. Their androgynous aesthetics challenged gender norms, while both engaged with sexual ambivalence: Bowie openly and Jackson through mystique. Each innovated visual storytelling, using persona and performance to push the boundaries of popular music culture and fashion.

They occasionally crossed paths at Studio 54 in the late 1970s and during Jackson's visits to Bowie's *Diamond Dogs* and *Serious Moonlight* shows in LA. In the 1980s, both featured in Pepsi commercials, their images repackaged and broadcast globally. Jackson was friends with Elizabeth Taylor, who had introduced Bowie to John Lennon. Each had a personal bond with Sean Lennon: Bowie became a father figure after John's death, while Sean was a frequent guest at Neverland Ranch and appeared in *Moonwalker*.

Their circles also overlapped musically and visually. Both drew on Beethoven's *Ninth Symphony*: Bowie opened his Ziggy Stardust concerts with Wendy Carlos' synth-driven adaptation from *A Clockwork Orange*, while Jackson framed 'Will You Be There' with its spiritual overtones. They collaborated with Mick Jagger, Nile Rodgers, Lenny Kravitz and Freddie Mercury, and were directed by John Landis and Martin Scorsese. Jim Henson considered Jackson for the role of the Goblin King in *Labyrinth* before his son Brian persuaded him to cast Bowie instead. 'Billie Jean' was made by Steve Barron, who also directed Bowie's 'Underground' and 'As The World Falls Down', while Mark Romanek, responsible for the videos for 'Jump They Say' and 'Black Tie White Noise', helmed Jackson's space-themed 'Scream'. Iman appeared as Jermaine Jackson's love interest in his 1985 video for 'Do What You Do', and in 1992, as Bowie's fiancée, she played the queen in Michael's pharaonic 'Remember The Time'. Bowie name-checks Jackson in Tin Machine's 'Shopping For Girls', and Bowie's name is listed under 'Special Thanks' in the end credits of Jackson's *Dangerous. The Short Films*. Even Joseph Merrick, the so-called Elephant Man, appears in both their narratives: Jackson was rumoured to have sought his remains, while Bowie embodied him on stage.

Bowie waited 20 years to give 'V-2 Schneider' its live debut, folding it into the drum 'n' bass set of the 1997 *Earthling Tour*. A driving live version was released that year as the B-side to 'Pallas Athena', credited to Tao Jones Index. Both tracks were recorded at Amsterdam's Paradiso on 10 June, in front of a 1,500-strong crowd. Meanwhile, just across town, 50,000 people were attending a Michael Jackson concert at the Amsterdam Arena. In *De Volkskrant*, Bowie voiced his respect for Jackson and empathy for what he saw as a lonely, pressured existence. He also expressed his joy at being able to perform a wilfully eccentric jungle set in an intimate club setting. Two global icons, one city, one hot summer night, each drawing power from a different kind of stage.

'Sense Of Doubt'

The opening scene shows Christiane staring blankly from a train window as the descending four-note piano motif tolls with the weight of a funeral bell: solemn, leaden, irreversible. The haunting minimalism of 'Sense Of Doubt' found its most public resonance not on a Bowie album, but in scenes of quiet devastation in *Christiane F. – Wir Kinder Vom Bahnhof Zoo*, a 1981 West German biographical drama directed by Uli Edel. It tells the story of Christiane Felscherinow, played by Natja Brunckhorst, a bored and alienated 13-year-old in 1970s West Berlin who descends into heroin addiction by the age of 14.

The film was based on the 1978 book *Wir Kinder Vom Bahnhof Zoo*, itself a shaped narrative drawn from tape-recorded interviews by the journalists Kai Hermann and Horst Rieck. Its title refers to Berlin's Zoologischer Garten station, which, during the 1970s and 1980s, was a notorious gathering place for the city's drug scene. Christiane's rapid slide into heroin use and prostitution at such a young age was shocking, serving as an unflinching warning that horrified many viewers. Both the book and the film were used in schools as stark cautionary tales about drug abuse, with Bowie's music as an existential backdrop.

A devoted Bowie fan, Christiane had attended his Berlin concert during the *Station To Station Tour* in 1976, where she had her first encounter with heroin. In a 2013 *Der Tagesspiegel* interview, Edel stated that Bowie's music was essential to the film and that it would have been unthinkable without him. According to the director, Bowie showed a genuine interest in the project, which helped secure the rights. 'Bowie's music *was* Berlin at that time', he told the BFI in 2017. To recreate Christiane's concert experience, Bowie agreed to appear in the film, performing 'Station To Station' using the live version from *Stage*. His scenes were filmed at New York's Hurrah nightclub in 1980, with only part of the cast and crew present, as Bowie was performing *The Elephant Man* on Broadway and unable to shoot in Berlin. The footage from the shoot at Hurrah, which also served as the location for the filming of Bowie's 'Fashion' video, was later spliced with crowd scenes from an AC/DC concert in West Germany to create the illusion of a single event.

Besides the live version of 'Station To Station', the film's soundtrack focuses on Bowie's Berlin-era music, driving Christiane's descent into Berlin's underworld. The scene of her and her friends vandalising a shopping centre to '"Heroes"' became one of the film's defining images. Yet

'Sense Of Doubt' is used to even more chilling effect, unfolding like a grainy documentary. As the piano tolls, the camera follows Christiane through the station's alleys, lingering on drug users slumped against stained underpass walls, many of them real-life Zoo regulars cast as extras. The track's eerie bleakness merges uncannily with the film's vérité style, capturing not just a girl's collapse but a city's.

The album's first true instrumental, since Bowie's altered voice still appears in 'V-2 Schneider', stands in sharp contrast to the often playful atmosphere in the studio between Bowie and Eno. 'We spent a lot of time laughing. Laughing at ourselves, at our pretentiousness and at some of the stuff that never got on to the album. It was rich with self-parody as well as a lot of inventive ideas', Bowie told *The Observer* in 1977. 'There's a sense of foreboding one wouldn't have expected to come out of that environment, but it did.' Entirely steeped in the Berlin myth that seeps through the album's reception, the unease on 'Sense Of Doubt' seems to reflect the city's oppressive, grey-toned appearance, as if the music had soaked up its atmosphere. 'It's not a relaxed place, certainly, and it produces a kind of nervous mirth, whistling in the dark', Bowie said of Berlin.

The track conjures the desolate expanse of Lichtenberg, U-Bahns pulling into fluorescent-lit platforms beneath a deserted Alexanderplatz, the wind echoing through tiled corridors at Storkower Straße station, concrete stairwells, shuttered kiosks and graffiti on walls. The four-minute piece is so sparse, associative and cinematic that it unfolds as a procession of imagery, each scene lining up behind the next: patrolling guards, searchlights sweeping the frosted soil of the death-strip, an unlit hallway with flickering overhead tubes stretching into blackness, an unmoving silhouette on a high-rise balcony, the hum of surveillance monitors behind reinforced windows, concrete watchtowers, distant dogs barking and skeletal trees clawing at the night sky.

In 1978, an early member of Einstürzende Neubauten and founding member of Mania D and Malaria!, Gudrun Gut, met Bowie at the opening of the SO36 club in Kreuzberg. She told *Electronic Sound* in 2018:

> I do think it was nice for Berlin that he was here because nobody cared about the city at that time. It was totally lost. A little island with a wall around us. There was no business here, the city was subsidised because it couldn't live by itself, and people outside were thinking, 'Why do we spend so much money on West Berlin? Let's just give it to the East.'

It echoes the title and atmosphere of 'Sense Of Doubt' with an almost eerie precision. The song came together through Eno's *Oblique Strategies*, a deck of cryptic prompts devised with Berlin-born artist Peter Schmidt, partly inspired by Edward De Bono's ideas on lateral thinking. Each card offered a gnomic suggestion designed to disrupt routine and provoke sideways moves.

'Emphasise the flaws.' 'Repetition is a form of change.' 'Honour thy error as a hidden intention.' Having already been used on *Low*, Eno only returned to the *Oblique Strategies* during the final phase of the *"Heroes"* sessions, when he and Bowie were shaping the instrumentals. The process sometimes led nowhere, but on 'Sense Of Doubt' it produced something striking. They drew a card in silence, following its direction without revealing it to the other. 'It was like a game', Eno told *Interview* in 1978. 'We took turns working on it; he'd do one overdub and I'd do the next. The idea was that each was to observe his *Oblique Strategy* as closely as he could.' Eno's card read 'Make everything as similar as possible', while Bowie's said 'Emphasise differences'. The unresolved tension between their opposing instructions is what lends the track its dark, fractured atmosphere.

The piano motif emerges beneath synthetic washes of wind and surf, while Bowie's keyboard chords rise in the spaces between. They arrive like the first glimmers of dawn, shafts of sunlight checked by the weight of the piano, which seems unwilling to surrender the darkness just yet. The higher phrases move like a tentative brass section threading through drifting mist, yielding at 1:45 to a plaintive lower sweep that folds in on itself sonically and invites a momentary truce with the piano's downward drag. Equilibrium soon gives way as the piano returns unrelentingly, accompanied by eerie traces: Bowie dragging a pick slowly across a guitar string, echoing the sound in his throat. It is a sonic detail mentioned by Visconti in *A New Career In A New Town*, the kind of memory that might make an instrumental purist shift in their seat. The track ends with howling wind, fading seamlessly into the Far Eastern drift of 'Moss Garden'.

Although the piece does not credit Eno as a co-writer, his influence on Bowie's writing is unmistakable. 'Eno helped me to relate to a working situation that had validity in itself – that wasn't just lost in pursuit of rock 'n' roll *status*', Bowie told *Newsday* in 1977. The following year, he told *Melody Maker*:

> He got me off narration, which I was so intolerably bored with. Narrating stories, or doing little vignettes of what at the time I thought was happening in America and putting it on my albums in convoluted fashion: Philadelphia, or New York, or LA, 'Panic In Detroit' and 'Young Americans'. Singer-songwriter askew. And Brian really opened my eyes to the idea of processing, to the abstract of communication.

Notably, Eno articulates a 'sense of doubt' in the liner notes to his 1978 album *Ambient 1: Music For Airports*, where he wrote: 'Whereas conventional background music is produced by stripping away all sense of doubt and uncertainty (and thus all genuine interest) from the music, Ambient Music retains these qualities.' A related idea appears in his 1996 book *A Year With Swollen Appendices*, where he argued that rationality is what we use to make the world predictable, while art is a rehearsal for the inapplicability and failure of that process. Doubt and confusion are no longer obstacles, but creative fuel: it is in that 'sense of doubt' that the space opens up for meaning and innovation. Seen from this perspective, the track becomes more than a mood piece: it is an artistic stance, one in which foreboding uncertainty is not resolved, but allowed to resound at the core.

During the 1977 studio shoot for the '"Heroes"' video, Stanley Dorfman also directed a little-seen promotional film capturing Bowie performing 'Blackout' and 'Sense Of Doubt'. Bowie later brought the latter to television, appearing in *Musikladen Extra* and *L'Altra Domenica*, and included it in the 1978 *Stage Tour*. When mixing the recordings for the live album *Stage*, Visconti chose to omit most of the audience noise during the performances, as crowd interruptions had occasionally disrupted the instrumental material from *Low* and *"Heroes"*. On his former official website, he mentioned that the audience became somewhat raucous during 'Sense Of Doubt', even noting a 'boo' at the start – a disturbance he felt marred the recording. In *Life On Tour With Bowie*, Sean Mayes, the tour's pianist, recalled a warmer reception: at the second show in Osaka, Japan, 'there was even applause for the start of 'Sense Of Doubt'!'

In *Ricochet*, the 1984 semi-documentary filmed during the Asian leg of Bowie's *Serious Moonlight Tour*, there is a brief yet hauntingly memorable sequence in which he wanders alone through an empty shopping mall, filmed at the Far East Plaza in Singapore. The shops are closed, the fluorescent lights cold and blue. Bowie moves silently on an escalator, shifting between levels without apparent purpose, while the sombre tones of 'Sense Of Doubt' pulse beneath him. His gaze is vacant, quietly reflective, as if he has slipped outside his own narrative for a moment. The next shot finds him sitting alone in the deserted concourse, flanked by white plastic Christmas trees. The imagery is both banal and poetic: a world of sleek modern consumerism, observed by someone who is present yet removed. He does not participate; he watches.

These scenes carry the same hollow stillness, visual dislocation and existential vacancy that permeate Sofia Coppola's *Lost In Translation*, the 2003 film starring Bill Murray and Scarlett Johansson. Their characters, Bob and Charlotte, are spiritually adrift in Tokyo. They speak none of the languages around them: not of the country, not of their partners, not even of themselves. They move slowly through neon-lit silence, drifting inward. In both *Ricochet* and Coppola's film, the modern Asian metropolis becomes a space where the self recedes. *Lost In Translation* could have been titled *Sense Of Doubt*.

In the similarly estranged world of *The Life Aquatic With Steve Zissou*, released in 2004, Murray wanders through pastel melancholy as Steve Zissou, while Bowie's music floats through the film in the form of acoustic Portuguese covers by Seu Jorge. In 2006, Bowie and Johansson shared the screen in *The Prestige*, directed by Christopher Nolan, who would later model Cillian Murphy's look in *Oppenheimer* on the Thin White Duke era.

On *Anywhere I Lay My Head*, Johansson's 2008 Tom Waits tribute album, Bowie contributed backing vocals to 'Fannin' Street' and 'Falling Down'. Waits himself performed at the wedding of Sofia Coppola and director Spike Jonze, who teamed up with Arcade Fire in 2011 to create a short film based on their 2010 concept album *The Suburbs*. Bowie had already performed with Arcade Fire at the 2005 Fashion Rocks benefit concert, resulting in the *Live At Fashion Rocks* EP, which features their joint versions of 'Wake Up' and 'Five Years'. He would return eight years later to contribute backing vocals to their 2013 single 'Reflektor', taken from the album of the same name.

To close in the spirit of white plastic Christmas trees: Bowie was a devoted fan of the Italian crime drama series *Gomorrah*, which he personally recommended to Sofia Coppola, even gifting her the full DVD box set. Knowing of his enthusiasm for *Peaky Blinders*, Murphy sent him a Shelby clan cap worn on set as a Christmas present. In return, Bowie posed for a photo wearing the cap, complete with razor blades tucked into the brim. In 2015, he sent *Peaky Blinders* screenwriter Steven Knight an early copy of *Blackstar* and asked if his music could be used in the series. In retrospect, the moment in episode five of season one when Murphy's character draws a small black star in a notebook and says, 'Black star day is the day we take out Billy Kimber and his men', carries a quietly suggestive charge.

From his love of *A Clockwork Orange* to the 'muggin' gangs' of 'Sweet Head', from 'Diamond Dogs' and 'Dirty Boys' to his final notes for *The Spectator*, a planned 18th-century underworld musical, Bowie had a fascination for street gangs. It is not hard to imagine that his final masterpiece may have taken some of its cues from the brutal elegance of *Peaky Blinders*. That 'Lazarus' appeared in a 2016 episode of the show feels like a poignant tribute in the year of his death.

'Moss Garden'

Asked in 1980 by *NME* about his fascination with Japan, Bowie said: 'For me, it's a physical representation – or I can read it in terms of that – of great new modern advances precariously balanced against an old, kind of mythological way of thinking and being.'

His long-standing affinity with Japanese culture was evident in the striking Ziggy Stardust and Aladdin Sane costumes designed by Kansai Yamamoto, which drew on Kabuki theatre. Bowie was introduced to Kabuki while studying mime with Lindsay Kemp in the 1960s, and later deepened that connection when Bandō Tamasaburō, the renowned *onnagata* actor, taught him the secrets of *kumadori* makeup. His engagement persisted over the years: from appearing in a kimono at the London premiere of *Just A Gigolo* and at the WKCR Benefit Concert at Carnegie Hall in New York, and referencing Kyoto in 'Move On', all in 1979, to incorporating Japanese lyrics delivered by actress Michi Hirota in 'It's No Game Pt. 1' in 1980, and releasing his Japanese-language version of 'Girls' in 1987. He also admired Japanese cinema, composer Toru Takemitsu and avant-pop bands such as P-Model, The Plastics and Sandii & The Sunsetz. He was a guest at the Kyoto home of writer and cultural host David Kidd, whose book *All The Emperor's Horses* would later appear on his list of 100 favourite books.

Bowie first visited the country on tour in April 1973 and spent time in Kyoto between concert dates. Among the places he explored was Saihō-ji, a Rinzai Zen temple famed for its moss garden: a two-tiered landscape with over 120 varieties of moss forming a rich green tapestry in subtly shifting shades. The garden left a quiet mark.

He returned to Japan several times in the years that followed. In 1978, he appeared on the Japanese TV show *Star Sen Ichy Ya*, and a year later shot a TV commercial for Takara Shuzo, a grain-based shōchū called Crystal Jun Rock, for which he provided the instrumental track 'Crystal Japan', originally titled 'Fujimoto San'. The location, a little-known Zen temple in northern Kyoto, was his own choice. 'We considered another temple, but Bowie, who knew Kyoto well, insisted on Shōden-ji', recalled Hosomi Yoshirō, then Deputy Mayor and later Chairman of Takara, in *Asahi Shimbun* in 2016. 'During the shoot, he stared at the garden and wept. I couldn't ask if it was the landscape or sadness. He was a delicate and pure person.' Bowie and Iman also spent part of their honeymoon in Kyoto in 1992, shortly after their wedding in Florence, Italy. He kept a pressed and dried chrysanthemum picked during that trip as one of his most treasured possessions until the end of his life. More than a destination, Japan remained an artistic and spiritual counterpart for Bowie.

Back in 1977, in the art nouveau apartment at Hauptstraße 155 in Berlin, Bowie had converted one room into a stark, white-walled studio. He filled it with easels, blank canvases and oil paints, producing numerous works. Among his many paintings was a portrait of Yukio Mishima, the Japanese novelist, actor and nationalist who led a civilian militia and committed ritual *seppuku* in 1970. Bowie felt an affinity with Mishima, seeing in him a kindred spirit, someone who understood identity as a series of masks rather than a stable essence. Mishima's use of masks, drawn from Noh theatre and explored in *Confessions Of A Mask*, resonated deeply with Bowie's own instinct to reinvent himself through shifting personas. Both artists recognised the idea of a creative void behind these masks, a fertile emptiness out of which new selves could emerge.

For Bowie, this was not just a theatrical strategy but a way to transcend the limits of being human, as he admitted in 1976 when he told *Rolling Stone*: 'I always had a repulsive need to be something more than human. I felt very, very puny as a human.' Mishima's extreme, uncompromising exploration of these themes made him one of Bowie's most valued writers. In 1994, he bought Eduardo Paolozzi's bronze sculpture *Yukio Mishima: Second Version*, which was auctioned at Christie's. On *The Next Day* from 2013, Mishima's name resurfaced in the closer 'Heat': 'Then we saw Mishima's dog/Trapped between the rocks/Blocking the waterfall'. Bowie also included *The Sailor Who Fell From Grace With The Sea* among his 100 favourite books.

Through an intricate lattice of cultural cross-pollinations that connect Bowie, Mishima and Japan, Nagisa Ōshima, who directed *Merry Christmas, Mr. Lawrence* in 1983 starring Bowie, also served as cultural consultant during the 1984 production of Paul Schrader's *Mishima: A Life In Four Chapters*. Two years earlier, Schrader had approached Bowie for the title track of his film *Cat People*, resulting in a collaboration with Giorgio Moroder. For Schrader's *Mishima* film, Bowie's long-term collaborator and *"Heroes"* album cover photographer Masayoshi Sukita shot portraits of the cast and production. Composer and self-proclaimed Eno fan Ryuichi Sakamoto was initially approached to score *Mishima*, though the final soundtrack was ultimately composed by Philip Glass, who would later release his symphonies based on *Low* and *"Heroes"* in the 1990s.

In *Merry Christmas, Mr. Lawrence*, Sakamoto played Captain Yonoi, a repressed, coded-homosexual camp commandant whose look and manner Ōshima modelled on Mishima. The film's haunting main theme, composed by Sakamoto, appears as 'Forbidden Colours' in its vocal version on the soundtrack album, a title referencing Mishima's 1951 novel of the same name. Coincidentally, Sakamoto's father was an executive at a major publishing house and was directly responsible for handling Mishima's work. Mishima's presence also reached Bowie through the artist Tadanori Yokoo, an acquaintance who knew Mishima personally and briefly appeared in Schrader's *Mishima* film. Yokoo designed the famous silkscreen poster *The Aesthetics Of End* for one of Mishima's essays, while his self-titled book landed on Bowie's favourite book list as well.

These Japanese strands weave occasional echoes through the Berlin sonic fabric of *"Heroes"*, from Sukita's cover photo taken in Tokyo to Bowie's own thoughts of settling in Kyoto after his Berlin period. The intertwined threads find clear expression in the line 'I'm under Japanese influence' in 'Blackout' and in the instrumental 'Moss Garden', 'probably the most peaceful thing I've ever written' as Bowie told *NMM* in 1979 during a conversation with Sakamoto. Bowie reflected:

> In Yukio Mishima's novel *Spring Snow*, the protagonist walked through a garden and noticed that the waterfall was not flowing. Upon closer observation, he found there was a dead dog stuck at the top of the waterfall. This, I think, is the best metaphor for the concept of 'the world'. Many of my works carry that feeling, too. It presents a perfectly common note, a perfectly normal piece of music, but it's somehow odd. Even those that seem extremely reasonable are distorted in a way – just like looking at things in a slightly cracked mirror.

This tension between surface calm and underlying unease shapes 'Moss Garden', lending its tranquil sound an unsettling, reflective depth. It recalls *Epsilon In Malaysian Pale* by Tangerine Dream founder Edgar Froese, who briefly hosted Bowie before he settled into his own apartment at Hauptstraße. Bowie told *Mojo* in 1997:

> There was an album that I loved by Edgar Froese, *Epsilon In Malaysian Pale*; it's the most beautiful, enchanting, poignant work, quite lovely. That used to be the background music to my life when I was living in Berlin.

Like *Epsilon*, 'Moss Garden' features distinctive, sampled sonic beds. Its ethereal soundscape sets Eno's electronic atmospheres against Bowie's plucked koto, lending the piece a human dimension rooted in nature. The choice of the traditional Japanese zither may also have been partly inspired by Neu!, who had used the instrument on their 1973 album *Neu! 2*. The track avoids a clear tonal centre, relying on shifting textures and loosely repeating koto figures to sustain its open, floating feel. Eno's synth washes here anticipate the ambient intro he would later perform on U2's 'Where The Streets Have No Name'. In *A New Career In A New Town*, Visconti commented on the track:

> With 'Moss Garden', Brian excelled himself with textures that imitated nature, atmospheric elements of distant thunder, wind, water and bird call, all originating from his manipulation of the Synthi. David played his Chamberlin sampler, the successor to the Mellotron.

Eno reflected on the session in a 1977 *NME* interview:

> David wanted to do a piece which was very descriptive, something I don't normally do, inasmuch as I usually start something and then say, 'Oh, that's what it is', and then follow that direction. But this was quite studied. David told me about this place in Kyoto called the Moss Garden, and then we just started to work. And, again, there was this very sloppy sort of technique – like, I was just playing around with this chord sequence on the Yamaha synthesiser, and I said, 'Give us a shout when you think it's long enough', you know, and sort of carried on. And then David looked at the clock and said, 'Yeah, that'll probably do', and we stopped. And, on the record, that's exactly where the piece ends. I find this very, very curious. It's so random somehow.

That same *random somehow* quality may be part of what makes it one of the album's most quietly underrated tracks, and Visconti's favourite instrumental on *"Heroes"*, another piece shaped by Eno's *Oblique Strategies*. In a 2006 BBC interview, Eno recalled pulling a card that read 'Change nothing and continue with immaculate consistency', while Bowie claimed to have drawn one that said 'Destroy everything'. In reality, no directive read exactly that; the closest instruction was:

> Destroy
> –nothing
> –the most important thing

With neither revealing their chosen card, that contradiction is etched into the track itself. There's a palpable tension between the textural synth tones and the instinctive, almost unpremeditated plucking of the koto, which evokes a playful amplitude within traditional meditation, a kind of esoteric, spiritual presence in a place that embodies introspection and purity. Yet this timeless solemnity is disturbed by the faint passing of a high-altitude aircraft, leaving thin white contrails slicing the sky above the imagined Zen garden. The intrusions drag us back to 1977, to modernity, to the cold reality of metal wings ferrying people into isolated West Berlin. Visconti's production is so deft that the distant plane becomes almost visual, making the listener question whether the sound occurs inside or outside the music itself. That, too, is the question Saihō-ji's Moss Garden poses about introspection: where does the inner world end and the external world intrude? The piece revolves around what Japanese aesthetics call *ma*: the resonant interval between sounds or gestures. That liminal tension shapes the space between koto and synth, between presence and absence. In 1968, two years before his death, Mishima described his experience in an F-104 fighter jet in the essay *Sun And Steel*:

> This silver tube floating in the sky was, as it were, my brain, and its immobility the mode of my spirit. The brain was no longer protected by unyielding bone but had become permeable, like a sponge floating on water. The inner world and the outer world had invaded each other, had become completely interchangeable.

Like Mishima's silver tube in the sky, 'Moss Garden' suspends the listener in a space where those realms merge, inviting us to inhabit that unsettling, beautiful ambiguity.

'Neuköln'

The tension, the Wall, the guards, the sense of division, a stray German word: Berlin runs through *"Heroes"* like a watermark. Yet across the entire Berlin trilogy, and on its siblings *The Idiot* and *Lust For Life*, the city is never mentioned by name. In Bowie's elegiac 2013 reflection on his Berlin years, 'Where Are We Now?', he recalls Potsdamer Platz, Nürnberger Straße, the Bösebrücke, the nightclub Der Dschungel and the KaDeWe department store.

On *"Heroes"*, the only place name that directly links to the city is Neukölln – and it is misspelt. This has led to speculation that Bowie was referring to the band Neu! and the city of Köln, a bit of a stretch given that Neu! were founded in Düsseldorf and neither of its members came from Köln.

Another possibility lies in the name's etymology: Neukölln derives from 'New Cölln', which in turn comes from 'Cöln' – later 'Köln' – itself rooted in the Latin *colonia*. Stripped to 'Neuköln', as Bowie spells it, the word edges closer to Köln and its colonial root, brushing up against the idea of a 'new colony'. It's a resonance that evokes the district's migrant community, or perhaps just a stray linguistic by-product.

Though Bowie once wrote 'Kreutzburg' instead of Kreuzberg in the semi-fictional diary pages of *Outside*, his earlier use of the correct Polish spelling 'Warszawa' suggests he could be deliberate about naming. The intentional use of non-standard spelling in 'The Hearts Filthy Lesson', 'Thru' These Architects Eyes' and "Tis A Pity She Was A Whore' points in the same direction. Then again, in the 'Where Are We Now?' video, Potsdamer Platz is misspelt, while Nürnberger Straße and Bösebrücke appear without their umlauts. So are we dealing with carelessness in 'Neuköln', or a deliberate tweak to suggest an impression of Neukölln rather than a literal portrait? Both are plausible: Bowie was never overly concerned with spelling, as the *David Bowie Is* exhibition made clear, yet he also treated his own material with care and affection. 'Totally possessed, totally inspired by his art,' *Lazarus* director Ivo van Hove recalled on *Zomergasten* in 2019, 'his music was something in which he expressed himself completely. Every song he ever wrote came from his life, his heart, his pores.'

That same care shapes the album's final instrumental, fading in with aircraft noise as the serene moss garden is left behind. It is arguably the most divisive track on the album, known for Bowie's saxophone performance, which at times can teeter on the comic edge. 'I had to work out a way of putting a Turkish modal thing into it', he told *Musician* in 1983. 'It was very hard for me to use that scale against the background, so that probably produced the humorous aspect.' Still, it belonged to his favourite sax pieces he ever recorded, saying: 'There's kind of a lot of Ornette Coleman at the end of it.' In *NME* in 1977, co-writer Eno recalled:

> We stayed late one evening and did that piece called 'Neuköln'. I liked that very, very much. I was very impressed by that. And I was trying to think what it was like in painting. There was a German school in Berlin at the beginning of the century called *Die Brücke* – an expressionist school. Very rough, tough strokes and they all have a mood of melancholy about them or nostalgia, as if they were painting something that was just disappearing. And all of that – the boldness of attack, the unplanned evolutionary quality of the images and the overall mood – reminds me of the way David works.

That mix of roughness and melancholic transience was not far from the reality outside the studio walls. The inner streets of Neukölln's namesake quarter, just south of Kreuzberg and within a short walk of Hansa Studio, were lined with soot-darkened 19th-century tenements, home to many Turkish *Gastarbeiter* families. Their cafés, kebab shops and import stores sat alongside corner pubs and discount stores, coal smoke hanging in the courtyards. During the Weimar Republic, the district had been a stronghold of the KPD, the Communist Party of Germany. Under Nazi terror, that reputation made it a target for especially heavy raids and arrests of political opponents, who were often executed by guillotine or hanging in Berlin-Plötzensee Prison. After Germany's division, Neukölln lay in West Berlin, bricked off from surrounding districts and losing much of its residential appeal. Lower rents drew large numbers of Turkish 'guest workers', who crowded into bleak concrete apartment blocks pressed against the Wall. Bowie told *Melody Maker* in 1977:

> Berlin is a city made up of bars for sad, disillusioned people to get drunk in. One never knows how long it is going to remain there. One fancies that it is going very fast. That's one of the reasons, sure, why I was attracted to the city. It's a feeling that I really tried to capture in the paintings, while I was there, of the Turks who live in the city. There's a track on the album called 'Neuköln', and that's the area of Berlin where the Turks are shackled in bad conditions. They're very much an isolated community. It's very sad. Very, very sad. And that kind of reality obviously contributed to the mood on both *Low* and *"Heroes"*.

On *Lodger*, Bowie would address the theme through the Middle Eastern-tinged reggae funk of 'Yassassin', its title a phonetic rendering of *yaşasın*, the Turkish exclamation meaning 'long live', which he had noticed scrawled on a wall. In the song's lyrics, he adopts the perspective of an everyday immigrant, defined by work and survival, where pride, disillusionment, confrontation and resolve coexist.

'We came from the farmlands/To live in the city' condenses a familiar migration arc into two lines. The tone is twofold: 'We walked proud and lustful/In this resonant world' conveys initial optimism and appetite for experience, while also hinting at an echoing emptiness. The narrator stands firm against a hostile social climate, refusing both the fight and the flight, determined not to lose his footing or sense of self. A staccato inventory follows, listing what he sees: the absence of warmth ('no value of love'), harshness ('just sun and steel', evoking Mishima's austere vision of the body and will) and indifference ('no second glances'). The pivot – 'then look at us' – sets up a sharp comparison between the migrant community and the cold, indifferent host society. This reality is underscored in 'Don't say nothing's wrong/I've got a love/And she's afeared'. Here, the social tension becomes personal, the abstract strain given a face in a vulnerable partner. The return to 'Yassassin' after these verses restores the song's centre: endurance. The refrain becomes a repeated statement of cultural pride and steadfastness, even within an environment of mistrust and marginalisation.

The delivery is forthright, voiced for public space, placing feelings, observations and defiance directly into the air. The looping groove lends the song a sense of daylight, as if someone keeps moving, working, carrying on, finding his rhythm with vitality while never blind to friction or threat. The conflict crystallises in 'You want to fight/But I don't want to leave/Or drift away', words that carry both spatial and emotional weight, touching on physical departure and an inner vanishing: a refusal to be swept away or detached from one's place, culture, or community. There is a troubling undertone of slowly sinking into anonymity or apathy, perhaps even forced assimilation.

Here, the chilly, desolate tones of 'Neukölln' cut in. Where 'Yassassin' embodies expressive endurance in daylight, 'Neukölln' turns inward to the nocturnal, tormented, estranged self: an impressionistic sonic rendering of a journey – the farm, the village, the promise of work in Germany and the harsh reality that replaced that dream. Suspended between two worlds, no longer at home in the country of origin, yet not fully accepted in the country of arrival. Eno's austere synths lay an unyielding canvas over which painterly squawking and howling strokes of Bowie's sax drift in modal curls, conjuring homesickness, dread and alienation before erupting into shrieking, keening cries.

In retrospect, its forlorn sorrow feels like a premonition. In the years ahead, Berlin's Turkish community would face renewed tensions: Chancellor Kohl's government openly discussed halving their numbers as 'culturally incompatible' with German life, followed by rising anti-immigrant sentiment and, by the early 1990s, violent attacks and murders committed by neo-Nazi groups.

The penultimate track of *"Heroes"* stands as a bold piece that sits powerfully within the album, though the playing never quite blooms into the momentum that Bowie's modal experiment seems to seek. Arresting in bursts, it falls short of the immersive pull such ambition promises. For those who find his avant-garde impulse here excessive, 'Neuköln' could just as well score a lone midnight motorway run, the saxophone doubling as the caffeine shot that keeps you from drifting into the crash barrier.

Close to the city streets that shaped the track's mood, Christiane F. grew up in a drab high-rise estate in Neukölln's southern reaches. Following the corrosive fame brought by *Wir Kinder Vom Bahnhof Zoo*, which turned her into an emblem of heroin's stranglehold on Berlin youth, she appeared in the 1984 German cyberpunk film *Decoder*, a jagged piece inspired by William S. Burroughs' essay *The Electronic Revolution*, with Burroughs himself in a cameo role. On the soundtrack was a band featuring her then-boyfriend:

Neukölln-born multi-instrumentalist Alexander Hacke of Einstürzende Neubauten, regulars at Hansa Studios. Their singer-guitarist, Blixa Bargeld, was living on Langenscheidstraße while Bowie and Iggy were on Hauptstraße, a short walk away, sharing the same streets and winter light.

Half a world away, a young Australian Bowie devotee, Nick Cave, was playing Bowie, Velvet Underground and Stooges covers with his friend Mick Harvey in The Boys Next Door. By 1980, the band had moved to London, renamed themselves The Birthday Party and plunged into a period of experimentation and savagery fuelled by heroin and internal friction. Too brutal for most audiences, they found refuge in 1982 in the crumbling bohemian hub of West Berlin, where Bargeld joined them shortly before the band collapsed. Nick Cave And The Bad Seeds emerged from the ashes, with Cave and Harvey at the core and Bargeld a constant presence. The Bad Seeds recorded multiple albums at Hansa, fusing their sound with the city's own. During those Berlin years, which included a stretch in Schöneberg near Bowie's former apartment, Cave, deeply addicted to heroin, stayed for several months with Christiane F., hiding from the press and trying to go cold turkey. In 1987, the band appeared as themselves in Wim Wenders' film *Der Himmel Über Berlin*. In one scene at the Lohmühlenbrücke, the sealed border crossing between Neukölln in West Berlin and Treptow in East Berlin, the Wall looms in the background, daubed with graffiti reading 'We Can Be Heroes'.

Nearly two decades later, in 2006, Bowie appeared in Wenders' short film *The World's Greatest Music Stores* for Nokia, speaking about his lifelong passion for discovering and sharing new music. In 2017, Mick Harvey served as musical director of the Australian *Bowie In Berlin* tribute tour, and in 2025, Bargeld released the EP *Blixa Bargeld Sings David Bowie*. In 2013, Cave told *Spex* of his admiration for Bowie's 'Where Are We Now?': 'What a wonderful song! I see Berlin before my eyes – the city of West Berlin that doesn't exist anymore. It only took all those names of places he sang, and my whole blurry time in Berlin passed before my inner eye again.'

A year later, Cave sang with Iggy on a cover of The Gun Club's 'Nobody's City', based on a demo for their album *Mother Juno*, recorded at Hansa in 1987. The record featured guitarist Kid Congo Powers, who would later name his own band The Pink Monkey Birds after 'Moonage Daydream'. Cave and Iggy were joined by Thurston Moore on guitar. Moore's band Sonic Youth had performed alongside Bowie at his 50th-birthday concert and had earlier proved a major influence on Tin Machine; 'Tom Violence' was one of Bowie's all-time favourite songs. Over the years, Einstürzende Neubauten, Iggy, Cave, Sonic Youth and Tin Machine all played Huxley's Neue Welt, a venue woven into the history of Berlin's underground and the shifting cultural frontiers in Neukölln.

'The Secret Life Of Arabia'

In 1977, the Middle East was firmly in the spotlight: the Lebanese Civil War, the Palestinian conflict and oil diplomacy dominated headlines. Yet in West

Berlin, the Arab community was small, made up mostly of students, diplomats, political refugees and a handful of migrant workers. Across the West, 'Arabia' remained largely a mirage, a fantasy shaped by perfume, film, fashion and exoticism. This funky track feels like a drift into that illusion, a sensual detour from the concrete melancholy of West Berlin.

Whether *"Heroes"* should have finished with the chill and desolation of 'Neukölln' remains a favourite debate among Bowie fans. That would have left the album with a stark, haunting finale, the last sound being Bowie's wailing saxophone. Yet there's a genuine shiver of anticipation the moment the guitar and congas of 'The Secret Life Of Arabia' slide in after the final shriek of 'Neukölln'. Once the skittish, half-mocking disco groove locks in, it plays like the album's own technicolour end credits roll.

'The Secret Life Of Arabia' is something of an overlooked Bowie album closer. An album-only track that rarely makes best-of lists, partly because he never played it live. A quiet loss because it stands as a strikingly enigmatic coda. At the same time, it gestures beyond the record: from *Low*'s retreat from LA paranoia to Bowie regaining his footing in Berlin, and towards the travel theme that would run through his next release.

The opening line, 'I was running at the speed of life', revisits 'Speed Of Life', the instrumental that opens *Low*. It is a phrase unlikely to be reused unintentionally, suggesting a deliberate closing note in a two-part arc, before *Lodger* was later folded into the Berlin trilogy. Themes of movement and change in Bowie's work run in parallel with his recurring references to film, alternative identities and constructed realities, from the 1969 mime piece *The Mask*, filmed as part of *Love You Till Tuesday*, to the cinematic illusions of 'Life On Mars?', which presents the silver screen as a futile antidote to grey drudgery. In 'Quicksand', the line 'I'm the twisted name on Garbo's eyes' evokes an identity built from image and interpretation rather than presence. In 'Five Years', the world is ending, yet it seems staged, as if he is merely an actor in a scene. Bowie always understood identity as a costume. On *Hunky Dory*, he even credited himself as co-producer under the name 'The Actor'.

On 'The Secret Life Of Arabia', this idea takes on a dreamlike dimension: 'you must see the movie' folds the scene in on itself, while 'I saw your eyes at the cross fades' frames the gaze as a splice between reverie and perception. Arabia becomes a stylised fiction, echoing the tradition of cinematic orientalist melodrama, with Bowie casting himself as the lead in a film that exists only in his own mind. That lineage stretches back to *The Sheik* from 1921, which made Rudolph Valentino a superstar and simmered with performative desire, masks and exoticism.

By the late 1970s, interest in Valentino flared up again, fuelled by a growing reappraisal of camp and silent film icons, and by the release of Ken Russell's biopic *Valentino* in 1977. In 1979, Iggy namechecks the actor in 'Don't Look Down', a track Bowie would revisit five years later on *Tonight*. *The Sheik* had set the template for the desert romance, crystallising tropes that later films would recycle and embellish. *The Desert Song* followed in 1929, complete with disguises, passion in the sand and Western longings projected onto a romanticised East. In 'The Secret Life Of Arabia', Bowie's warped allusion – 'I walk through a desert song when the heroine dies' – recasts the desert theatrics as fatal, as if the operetta veil finally drops to reveal death beneath.

The Sheik and *The Desert Song* had long depicted the desert as a backdrop for longing and operetta fantasy. A 1943 remake of *The Desert Song* reframed the setting as a patriotic battleground, turning it into a new kind of arena for anti-Nazi adventure. In David Lean's 1962 epic *Lawrence Of Arabia*, starring Peter O'Toole, the desert became something else entirely: an inner landscape, arid, unforgiving and morally elusive. The film recounts the story of British Intelligence Officer T. E. Lawrence, who fought alongside Arab guerrilla forces during the First World War. That mystique lingers in the detached atmosphere of 'The Secret Life Of Arabia', tinged with cryptic suggestion. The song title nods to *The Secret Lives Of Lawrence Of Arabia*, a 1960 biography that openly explores Lawrence's hidden homosexuality, self-mythologising and the divide between his public persona and private trauma. The notion of an outsider reinventing identity within a foreign culture fits seamlessly with Bowie's own fascinations and with his status at the time, pursuing a new career in a new town.

The association returned visually in 1983, both in *Merry Christmas, Mr. Lawrence* and during the *Serious Moonlight Tour*. With his suntanned skin and bleached blond hair, Bowie bore more than a passing resemblance to O'Toole's Lawrence, while on stage Carlos Alomar even wore a costume recalling the tales of *One Thousand And One Nights,* a trope also faintly evoked a decade earlier in the punning name Aladdin Sane. The year after the tour, in the *Jazzin' For Blue Jean* video, Bowie appeared as a kind of Arab princeling, another echo of Lawrence's mythic desert aura. O'Toole, incidentally, was once considered for the lead in *The Man Who Fell To Earth* before the ultimate outsider role went to Bowie himself, who in the early 1980s was even offered the part of Lawrence in a planned remake.

The reference runs deeper still. The real T. E. Lawrence features prominently in Colin Wilson's *The Outsider*, a book Bowie included in his list of 100 favourite books and cited as a formative influence in his youth. Wilson's study explores the 'outsider' in literature and philosophy, focusing on figures such as Lawrence, Van Gogh, Nietzsche and H. G. Wells, all of whom wrestled with alienation from mainstream society. He also discusses T. S. Eliot and Camus, who, like Wilson, appear in Bowie's list, as well as Harley Granville-Barker, author of the play *The Secret Life*, aptly enough. Lawrence himself admired the play, writing to Granville-Barker in 1923 that it was 'a very great thing', a reminder that even within Wilson's constellation these figures were connected. Bowie's characters – from Ziggy to Halloween Jack to the Duke, and even his greyscale Berlin incarnation – are elusive outsiders themselves, poised at the edge of society or moving between man and myth, much like Wilson's archetypes.

It all leads to a beguiling closing track, veiled in the dusky shimmer of an imagined Arabia, a projection of desire that drifts just beyond grasp. The secret life is 'evergreen': untouched, never withering, because it's never lived. That single word carries a quiet, piercing ambiguity: the sorrow of what remains intact by staying forever out of reach, and the faint purity that clings to what is never seized.

The song's celluloid charge lingers as a desert-borne phantasm, wrapped in an effortlessly gliding groove. Co-writer Alomar cuts tight against the beat with a funk-tinged, textural part, all subtle syncopation and breathing room between crisp strokes. He adds a second line that slips in like a shadow, nudging transitions and flicking little sparks across the track. Eno told *NME* in 1977:

> David would say, 'Okay, it's that, that, twice as long on that, and then that, and we do this a couple of times and then back to that again.' And after that very brief instruction, we'd start playing, and in that tiny space of time, Carlos would have worked out this lovely line. He's quite remarkable. He gives those pieces a lot of character.

Bowie's renewed confidence at the piano had been forged through his playing on *The Idiot* and *Lust For Life* and honed night after night on tour with Iggy. His playing here has a loose, infectious swing, reminiscent of Andrea True Connection's 'More, More, More', while Murray's supple disco bassline lands a fifth beat that hangs just enough to make it tight yet deliciously laid back. Looking back in *Guitar World* in 2026, Murray said:

> I don't remember what possessed me to come up with that line. I was just reacting to the chords, and channelling everything I'd learned to that point. The rhythm is clearer than it is on other tracks; there's a separation, so you can really feel the bass and the drums moving the song forward. Even though we sped up a tiny bit at the end due to excitement, my concept was to play the part right in the middle of the pocket, because that's how David presented the song.

Davis opens with supple, earthy congas before sliding into dry, controlled drumming, spiced with subtle snare ghost notes. As he is throughout the album, Bowie is in great voice, stringing out the title phrase over an octave jump and savouring every syllable. Eno's sweeping synth lines spill across the track with cinematic flair, touched by a campy hint of soft-focus kitsch – as do Maass' backing vocals. The moment those handclaps burst in at 1:52, just after Bowie sings 'when the heroine dies', is disarmingly simple yet impossible to resist. For more of that funky vibe, The Gap Band's 'Oops Upside Your Head' and Ian Dury's 'Inbetweenies' and 'Hit Me With Your Rhythm Stick' make perfect follow-ups.

East Berlin-born punk provocateur and actress Nina Hagen performed 'Ziggy Stardust' on *The Old Grey Whistle Test* in 1980. Two years later, on her album *NunSexMonkRock*, the track 'Iki Maska' briefly quoted from the same song. During the tour that followed, she folded 'The Secret Life Of Arabia' into her set, performing it with her trademark baroque fervour. Billy MacKenzie's equally eccentric reinterpretation with the British Electric Foundation also appeared in 1982, teasing out the sleek sensuality of Bowie's original with theatrical urgency. The Associates, MacKenzie's band, had debuted in 1979 with an unauthorised cover of 'Boys Keep Swinging', released just weeks after Bowie's original, a bold move that led to a deal with Bowie's publishers and a proper record contract. Years later, his haunting take on 'Wild Is The Wind' was released posthumously after his death by suicide in 1997. Like Bowie and T. E. Lawrence, MacKenzie moved through life steeped in ambiguity: elegant, elusive and drawn to both sexes yet resistant to fixed definition. All three crafted layered personae that blurred the lines of identity, sexuality and cultural belonging, inviting fascination as much as projection. The true secret life of Arabia.

'Abdulmajid' (Bonus Track)

'Abdulmajid' is a cryptic Bowie-Eno instrumental, its origins shrouded in speculation. The *"Heroes"* Rykodisc CD reissue credits place it around 1976-79, though no official session logs confirm that dating. Its Middle Eastern undertones echo faint traces of 'Neuköln' and 'The Secret Life Of Arabia', which could suggest a holdover from the tail end of the Berlin recordings. In *The Complete David Bowie*, Visconti recalls it as an untitled abandoned track from the *"Heroes"* sessions. However, since there is no public record of registration before 1991 with BMI or any other rights organisation, it cannot be entirely ruled out that the piece was a new recording, mischievously presented by Bowie as a lost Berlin-era outtake. The same ambiguity surrounds 'I Pray, Olé', a *Lodger* bonus track that may just as easily be an actual overdubbed outtake as a post-facto pastiche, consistent with Bowie's enduring delight in playful fabrication and staged credibility.

Meeting Lou Reed backstage after a Velvet Underground show in 1971 had been a thrill for Bowie, and he left the venue elated. Only later did he discover it had been Doug Yule all along, who had stepped in for Reed the previous year and played along. Bowie was far from embarrassed: he found the imposture delightful, entirely in line with his taste for blending projection and reality.

In 1973, when Roxy Music opened for him at the Greyhound in Croydon, Bowie met Eno for the first time. Eno asked whether he had ever considered sending a completely different band onstage to impersonate Ziggy and The Spiders without informing the audience, and Bowie knew at once he wanted to work with him someday. That same taste resurfaced in 1998, when Bowie helped launch a hoax biography of the fictional artist Nat Tate, concocted with author William Boyd. At an April Fools' Day gathering of New York art insiders, Bowie claimed to own one of Tate's paintings and read excerpts from the book aloud, fooling many of the notables who nodded along in apparent recognition.

Whatever its true provenance, 'Abdulmajid' was mixed by Bowie and Dave Richards in 1991, with added overdubs. It was released that year as a bonus track, a year after Bowie had met and fallen for Iman Abdulmajid, whom he would marry in 1992. Although Bowie titled it after her, sonically it's far from a sweeping romantic gesture: a three-note synthesiser motif pulses over an industrial rhythm track, cloaked in ambient haze and spectral noise. More haunted corridor than honeymoon suite.

In 1996, 'Abdulmajid' became part of Philip Glass' *Symphony No. 4: Heroes*, his second orchestral reimagining of the Berlin trilogy, following *Symphony No. 1: Low* from 1992. Glass recalled in a 1993 interview with *The Independent* that Bowie and Eno had both, independently, attended his 1971 concert at the Royal College of Art. Not long after, Bowie got in touch, and the two met at the Peppermint Lounge in New York: Bowie already a star, Glass still driving a cab. It was the beginning of a mutual admiration that would endure for decades. The robotic backing vocals on 'Loving The Alien' from 1984 were inspired by *Einstein On The Beach*. In the 1990s, Bowie would record significant parts of *Earthling* and *Toy* at Looking Glass Studios, the Manhattan facility Glass had founded. Between 2001 and 2003, Bowie performed at the Glass-curated Tibet House Annual Benefit Concerts at Carnegie Hall in New York, with Glass himself playing piano on 'Space Oddity' in 2002. The composer felt a deep affinity with Bowie and Eno's artistic approach, describing *Low* and *"Heroes"* as modern classics of popular music. In the programme note for the *Heroes* symphony, he reflected:

> Twyla Tharp, the American choreographer with whom I had collaborated on the dance work *In the Upper Room*, suggested I think of *Heroes* as a ballet score for her new dance company. We suggested this to David, who immediately shared Twyla's enthusiasm for the idea. Accordingly, I set *Heroes* as a six-movement work, each movement based on a theme from the album, with an overall dramatic structure that would be suitable for dance. The result was a symphonic ballet – a transformation of the original themes combined with new material of my own and presented in a new dramatic form.

The symphony premiered in London in 1997, performed by the Academy of St Martin In The Fields. Soon after the release of a recording with the American Composers Orchestra, Bowie used the *Heroes* symphony as walk-in music at some of his live shows. He and Glass remained friends and continued to exchange creative ideas. After Bowie's death in 2016, he spoke to *The Guardian* about Bowie and Eno:

> He and Brian had an amazing creative partnership. I actually never knew who did what. Both were so gifted in their ability to write lyrical music. They told me, though, that they never worked together at the same time. They worked in the same studio, but one of them had the day hours, the other the evening hours. I don't even know how well they knew each other – I never actually saw them together!

As early as 1997, Glass had expressed his intention to write a third symphony and discussed possible approaches with Bowie. *Symphony No. 12: Lodger*, based on the album's lyrical content and met with a muted critical response, premiered in 2019, with the LA Phil and Angélique Kidjo as vocal soloist. Her Grammy-winning 2008 album *Djin Djin* was produced by Visconti, and in 2018, she released a full album reinterpretation of *Remain In Light* by Talking Heads, a record originally produced by Eno. Interesting as they are, Glass' symphonic reworkings refract Bowie's material through a different vocabulary and amplify its architecture, but in filing down its experimental grain, they lose some of the dramatic logic and emotive charge that gave the originals their force.

Bowie's own 'Abdulmajid' also appeared on both editions of *All Saints*, a compilation of his instrumental work. The first, a two-disc set, gathered pieces from *Low*, *"Heroes"*, *Black Tie White Noise* and *The Buddha Of Suburbia*, plus 'Some Are' from Glass' *Low* symphony. The *"Heroes"* pieces 'Sense Of Doubt', 'Moss Garden' and 'Neuköln' ran together as a single track. Bowie reportedly had 50 copies made as Christmas gifts for friends in 1993, personally selecting the tracklist. Another hundred were produced for promotional use, a small run that soon became a collector's prize.

In 2001, Virgin/EMI issued *All Saints: Collected Instrumentals 1977-1999*. The *Black Tie White Noise* selections and 'South Horizon' from *The Buddha Of Suburbia* were dropped, replaced by 'Brilliant Adventure' from *hours...* and the Japan-only single 'Crystal Japan', which had resurfaced in 1992 on Rykodisc's reissue of *Scary Monsters*. The title track 'All Saints', no less enigmatic in origin than 'Abdulmajid', had first appeared as a bonus track on *Low* in 1991. Its name tipped the hat to Eno's All Saints label, founded that same year and named after All Saints Road in Notting Hill. 'Abdulmajid' turned up again on another elusive piece for collectors in 2001: a five-track CDR, privately issued and signed by Bowie, included with early copies of *I Am Iman*. Only 200 were made, featuring 'Abdulmajid', 'The Wedding', 'Wild Is The Wind', 'Loving The Alien' and 'As The World Falls Down'.

The track's repeated resurfacing suggests more significance than it warrants: it has an early 1990s sheen of programmed darkness, with the tight, sequenced pulse of early electronic club music, slightly jarring against the pre-digital landscapes of *Low* and *"Heroes"*. Where those albums feel sealed inside a world before the fall of the Wall, 'Abdulmajid' and 'All Saints' seem to step straight into the years after, as if the tracklist had suddenly leapt a decade. Their Arabic inflections, coloured by a more clinical, synthetically shaped sound world, place them as satellites to the Berlin era rather than part of its core. It makes an apt pairing: both carry obscure, faintly suspect backstories and share a sonic palette that edges toward the industrial-ambient ground Bowie would later chart more boldly on *The Buddha Of Suburbia*, *Outside* and *Earthling*. If nothing else, both tracks can be seen as tentative forays into that terrain, from the metallic liturgy of 'Sex And The Church' to the scorched electronics of 'Law (Earthlings On Fire)'.

'Joe The Lion' 1991 Remix (Bonus Track)

Located inside the Montreux Casino, just steps from Lake Geneva, Mountain Recording Studio had played host to a remarkable cast: Led Zeppelin, Yes, AC/DC, The Stones and, of course, Queen, who took full ownership in 1979. The same casino had famously gone up in smoke during a Frank Zappa concert in 1971, immortalised in Deep Purple's 'Smoke On The Water'. David 'Dave' Richards was a British producer and engineer who made the studio his base from the late 1970s through the early 2000s. Quietly exacting behind the desk, Richards became a trusted collaborator to both Queen and Bowie. He served as assistant engineer on *"Heroes"*, with the final mix completed at Mountain by Bowie and Visconti. He co-produced *Never Let Me Down*, *The Buddha Of Suburbia* and *Outside*, and engineered the spontaneous 1981 Montreux session that led to 'Under Pressure'. From 'When The Wind Blows' to *Blah-Blah-Blah*, the 1986 Iggy album co-produced with Bowie, Richards remained Bowie's go-to studio partner throughout the Swiss years.

At the start of this period, Bowie's relationship with RCA had already soured, long before their contract ended in 1982. The label had embraced his ascent from *Ziggy Stardust* to *Young Americans*, but recoiled at *Low* and all but gave up by the time *"Heroes"* arrived. In the US, Bowie did not chart again until 'Fashion' in 1980. RCA continued to exploit his back catalogue, issuing stopgap compilations such as *Christiane F.*, *Changestwobowie* and *Rare*, all without his involvement. By 1983, Bowie had signed with EMI and released *Let's Dance*, which became a global success through MTV exposure, major-label promotion and the *Serious Moonlight Tour.* RCA responded with cash-in anthologies like *Fame And Fashion* and *Golden Years*, the latter featuring 'Joe The Lion', recycling old material with recent tour photos but no access to his current work.

Then came the CD. Although RCA showed little faith in the format, it issued most of Bowie's catalogue in early 1985 before its rights expired in 1988. The discs were rushed, poorly mastered from cassette-equalised tapes and cheaply packaged. Yet Bowie became one of the first major artists with a near-complete catalogue on compact disc. As the format exploded and demand outstripped supply, Bowie's RCA albums quietly vanished. His records were out of print and his legacy scattered. By the end of the 1980s, the rights to his pre-1983 catalogue had reverted to him, and he partnered with Rykodisc to reissue the albums on CD.

The campaign officially launched in September 1989 with the release of the *Sound+Vision* box set, followed in early 1990 by the global greatest hits tour of the same name. Between 1989 and 1992, Rykodisc followed up with newly remastered editions of every studio album from *Space Oddity* through *Scary Monsters*. Aside from variant inlay photos, what set these Ryko editions apart was the inclusion of bonus tracks personally selected by Bowie. Some were familiar B-sides and non-album singles, but the real appeal lay in unreleased material: outtakes, abandoned sketches and alternate mixes that have rarely resurfaced since. Highlights included 'Candidate (Demo)' on *Diamond Dogs*, 'It's Gonna Be Me' on *Young Americans* and 'Some Are' on *Low*.

Alongside 'Abdulmajid', a remixed version of 'Joe The Lion' by Richards appeared on the 1991 Ryko reissue of *"Heroes"*. It replaced the original's abrasive textures with a rigid late-1980s production style, hollowed out by a gated, overmixed drum track that flattened the song's original dynamics, and added reverb on Bowie's vocal. Its metronomic precision and processed sheen aligned it with the 1988 industrialised reworking of 'Look Back In Anger', released on the Ryko edition of *Lodger*. That overhaul had been used to great effect in the theatrical aggression of Bowie's dance routines with Louise Lecavalier from La La La Human Steps during his performance at Intruders at the Palace in July 1988. This version of 'Joe The Lion', however, can safely be consigned to the same corner of oblivion as the single edit of '"Heroes"'. What made the remix especially jarring was not just its sterile surface, but how it drained the original of its volatility, turning an unstable cry into a lifeless, mechanised echo.

For many fans encountering *"Heroes"* for the first time on Rykodisc CD, the two bonus tracks carried a strange, uninvited charge. They added nothing to the album's original impact and offered an unwelcome coda, like a note added after the fact. Later editions restored the album to its intended tracklist, leaving the bonus material behind. And now we kind of miss them.

From the ten songs on *"Heroes"*, three were never performed live: 'Neukölln', 'Moss Garden' and 'The Secret Life Of Arabia'. Always a borderline case in Bowie's live repertoire, 'Joe The Lion' was rehearsed for the *Stage Tour* in 1978, but ultimately not performed until the first two dates of the 1983 *Serious Moonlight Tour*. It was considered again for the 1987 *Glass Spider Tour*, but did not make the final setlist. It returned on the 1995 *Outside Tour* in a version closer to the original than the 1991 remix, resonating directly with the album's preoccupation with ritualised body art, in what would be its final live appearance.

The Sleeved Self

A few months before the *"Heroes"* sessions began, RCA released *The Idiot*. In April 1977, after wrapping its tour, Iggy and Bowie travelled to Tokyo to promote the album, with Bowie making only a passing reference to *Low*. During an impromptu session in a small Harajuku studio, Japanese photographer Masayoshi Sukita captured the image that would become the iconic *"Heroes"* cover, along with a portrait later used for Iggy's 1981 album *Party*, all within two hours and six rolls of film. Sukita told *Time* magazine in 2015:

> They called me up for an hour photo shoot each, so it didn't start off as an album cover; it was just a general photo session. I didn't think of any creative settings for David; everything just came out of the nature of David – he was just sitting or standing, or making a move. Then I realised, taking a portrait as a natural being was more interesting than making a creative setting. Instead of giving him directions, I just captured the nature of Bowie. I sent a bunch of contact sheets I picked to David, and a month later, he told me that they'd use that photo as the album cover. I was really happy about it.

Born in Fukuoka in 1938, Sukita developed a passion for music and visual culture early on. His father had died in the war, and despite their poverty, his mother managed to buy him a Rolleiflex camera, sparking his serious commitment to the medium. After graduating from the Japan Professional School of Photography and training under Shisui Tanahashi, he moved to Tokyo in 1965 and began working in fashion and advertising. Inspired by Woodstock, he became fascinated with Western subcultures and travelled as a freelance photographer to New York and London. In 1972, while in London to shoot Marc Bolan, Sukita spotted a poster for the Save the Whale concert, featuring Lou Reed, Marmalade, JSD Band and a certain *cat from Japan*. 'Back in the day, there was very little information available on David Bowie in Japan, and I had never even heard his name until I visited London. But the moment I saw him, I became extremely curious about him', Sukita recalled on the official Bowie website in 2013.

Struck by the concert, he set out to photograph the flame haired alien, contacting Bowie's management to show his portfolio and propose a session. The images made an impression, sparking a partnership that would last over 40 years, including the 1989 cover for *Tin Machine* and several acclaimed photo books. Their most enduring image remains the *"Heroes"* portrait, boldly repurposed for *The Next Day* in 2013. Shortly before the session, picking up on the new punk aesthetic, Bowie asked Sukita to arrange some leather jackets, a task taken on by stylist Yasuko 'Yacco' Takahashi. The resulting look, casually assembled, would go on to define the now-iconic imagery of the album cover and the '"Heroes"' video.

As often noted, Bowie's hieratic pose, one hand to the chest, the other raised, was inspired by Erich Heckel's painting *Roquairol* (1917), which also influenced the cover of *The Idiot*. Heckel's 1912 painting *Zwei Männer Am Tisch* (also known as *Dostojewski*) is generally understood to depict the charged encounter between Prince Myshkin and Rogozhin from the novel *The Idiot*, tightening the network of associations around Bowie's visual borrowing. He told *Uncut* in 1999:

> Since my teenage years, I had obsessed over the angst-ridden, emotional work of the expressionists, both artists and filmmakers, and Berlin had been their spiritual home. This was the nub of the *Die Brücke* movement, Max Reinhardt, Brecht and where *Metropolis* and *Caligari* had originated. It was an art form that mirrored life not by event but by mood. This was where I felt my work was going.

Heckel was a German painter and printmaker, and a founding member of *Die Brücke*, the expressionist group that pushed bold colour, jagged forms and visceral woodcuts into early 20th-century art. Their work aimed to reclaim emotional immediacy in a world of growing alienation and spiritual drift.

During the First World War, he served as a Red Cross medic in Flanders, an experience that left a deep mark on his work. In the 1930s, the Nazi Party labelled his art 'degenerate', confiscated it from museums and barred him from exhibiting. In 1944, most of his print blocks, plates and stored works were destroyed in a bombing raid, fittingly, in Berlin. After the war, he continued to paint and, for a time, taught at the Karlsruhe Academy, quietly rebuilding his life and artistic legacy until his death in 1970, aged 86. His work left a deep impression on Bowie, who noted in the same *Uncut* interview: 'Heckel's *Roquairol* and also his print from 1910 or thereabouts called *Young Man* was a major influence on me as a painter.' He also confirmed *Roquairol* as the source for the *"Heroes"* pose, dismissing claims it was based on a Walter Gramatté self-portrait: 'I personally couldn't stand Gramatté. He was wishy-washy in my opinion.' In 1977, Bowie acquired a Heckel woodcut print of *White Horses* (1912) from Galerie Warschau on the Kurfürstendamm, and later, with characteristic cheek, told the director of the Brücke-Museum that his copy was of better quality than the museum's.

Roquairol, one of Heckel's best-known works and an icon of German Expressionism, shows a young man with an intense, melancholy gaze rendered in harsh contrasts and unnatural colours. The painting has also been read as a kind of performative bearing, emphasising artifice over naturalism – an aesthetic Bowie likely found compelling, and subtly mirrored in his own framing gesture. The model was Heckel's friend and fellow Brücke artist Ernst Ludwig Kirchner, whose life was marked by psychological instability, morphine addiction, repeated stays in sanatoria and a death by gunshot, widely presumed to have been suicide.

Traumatised by his experiences during World War I, including a severe nervous breakdown, Kirchner channelled his inner turmoil into a visual language that shifted from jagged angularity to softer, more stylised clarity. Notably, he had depicted Bowie's future Berlin neighbourhood in works such as *Straße Am Stadtpark Schöneberg* and *Gasometer In Schöneberg*. His role as a troubled outsider echoes that of the tormented Romantic antihero Roquairol in Jean Paul's novel *Titan* (1800–1803), from which the painting takes its title.

This layered interplay of mask and self would later find striking form in Bowie's 1980 Broadway role in *The Elephant Man*, where he embodied the disfigured Joseph Merrick – referred to in the script as John Merrick – without prosthetics, revealing embodiment itself as a performed identity. His turn as the existential lead in the 1982 BBC adaptation of Brecht's *Baal* further deepens the dramaturgical logic behind the *"Heroes"* tableau. Bowie's fixed posture and detached stare echo not just Heckel's *Roquairol*, but also Brecht's Epic Theater, with its distancing masks, theatrical artifice and the notion of self as staging. The gesture also recalls a ritual from traditional Japanese Noh theatre, where actors would contemplate the mask before them, preparing to shed their identity and assume another.

Alongside *Roquairol*, other works that may have shaped Bowie's stance, given their resemblance, include Heckel's woodcuts *Männerbildnis*, *Mann In Der Ebene* and the *Roquairol* variations, as well as *Bildnis Des Dichters Frank* by Kirchner himself. Whatever image Bowie had stored in his mind to draw from, the chosen photograph is unmistakably akin to the expressionist idiom he had studied so closely and cherished so deeply. Echoes also appear in the stigmata of the ants-in-hand image from *Un Chien Andalou*, in the photographs of Egon Schiele by Anton Josef Trčka and in Schiele's own contorted, dystonia-like self-portraits: an aesthetic Bowie would further explore on the *Lodger* album cover. In 1978, he was even lined up to play Schiele in *Wally*, a planned film by Clive Donner with Charlotte Rampling as Wally Neuzil, though the project collapsed for lack of funding. On *"Heroes"*, the tension turns inward. Bowie channels the mood of European noir – Wenders, Fassbinder, Melville – coolly detached and tightly framed, brimming with restrained menace. An androgynous Elvis android, he stands frozen, a hero without heroism, like Delon in *Le Samouraï* or Hopper in *The American Friend*, trapped in a city of neon and rain.

The graphic design, executed by RCA's in-house design department with Bowie providing conceptual input, is radical and restrained: bold geometric sans-serif lettering enclosed in quotation marks, with a high-contrast black-and-white portrait that dominates the image, stripped of background detail. One unconventional choice is the title's placement. Rather than appearing in the expected top-left corner, free from distraction, it seems to collide deliberately with Bowie's raised fingers. The typography does not float above the image but locks into it, becoming part of a tense, angular frame that heightens the graphic tension, like a constructivist composition. An earlier mockup showed the letters in a handwritten capital font on Bowie's raised hand, lettering he would return to on the sleeve of *Scary Monsters*.

The back cover features stark, centred white text on black, echoing the album's austere, minimalist aesthetic. The Bauhaus ideal looms large: form follows function, free of flourish, reduced to elemental clarity, while the spirit of *Neue Sachlichkeit* lingers, too, marked by emotional detachment. This formal clarity carries across the entire sleeve, linking text and image through a shared graphic discipline. Form and tone converge: cool and composed, yet quietly taut. Given Bowie's fascination with Fritz Lang, the visual echo is unmistakable. Lang's early work is rooted in German Expressionism, with its pronounced contrasts and theatrical stillness. As in *Metropolis* and *M*, hand gestures become symbols, bodies become graphic signs. Bowie emerges as an Expressionist archetype: sculptural and alienated, a modern Mabuse or angular automaton, poised to enter eternity as pure style.

Signals In The Afterglow

By the autumn of 1977, Bowie had long become more than a pop star, more than a cult figure. He was a generative force. From Ziggy Stardust onward, he had redrawn the map for what a musician could be: visually, sexually, conceptually. A whole generation had tuned in to 'Starman' on *Top Of The Pops* and gone away with the sense that being different was not just allowed, but electrifying. Five years later, his signal had spread into dozens of new directions. Punk had claimed him as a patron saint, and a wave of new artists were already tuning in to the cooler transmissions of *Low,* his example still echoing across art schools and bedroom mirrors. He had been creative license, permission to escape and the promise of transformation. Whether it was the band name Warsaw, a lifted riff from 'Fame', or the fragmented electronics of *Low*, Bowie's imprint remained embedded across the cultural fabric.

When RCA released *"Heroes"* on 14 October, the day Bing Crosby died, the world of popular music was on edge. In the UK, punk was burning hot: The Sex Pistols were days away from releasing their only studio album, *Never Mind The Bollocks.* On the streets, in clubs and fanzines, the old guard of rock, glam and pop was under fire as never before. The provo spirit shaped by Malcolm McLaren and Vivienne Westwood, channelled by Johnny Rotten, brought three-chord distortion and an attitude that was defiant and polarising.

For Bowie in Berlin, the explosion felt distant: 'The few punk bands that I saw in Berlin struck me as being sort of post 1969 Iggy, and it seemed like he'd already done that', he told *Uncut* in 1999. Both his status and his exile had kept him off the radar, away from the scrutiny fellow fossils were facing back in the UK. His alliance with Iggy, who was now increasingly credited as punk's true precursor, and the genre-defying direction of *Low* had placed him in a different category altogether. RCA leaned into that position with slogans like 'Tomorrow Belongs To Those Who Can Hear It Coming' and 'There's Old Wave, There's New Wave And There's David Bowie'.

At the same time, mellow pop, disco and smooth radio rock were thriving in the mainstream. In the US, hits like 'You Light Up My Life' by Debby Boone and KC & The Sunshine Band's 'Keep It Comin' Love' soundtracked radio and clubs. Disco drums, lavish orchestration and dancefloor rhythms filtered through the underground, the top 40 and prime-time TV. Above it all floated the runaway success *Rumours* by Fleetwood Mac, the glossy face of emotional soft rock, saturating the airwaves. In the UK, the charts were a mixed bag. Punk screamed next to hits like 'Yes Sir, I Can Boogie' by Baccara and La Belle Epoque's 'Black Is Black', tracks driven by disco pulses and light pop groove. Traditional rock and pop acts like Rod Stewart, 10cc and posthumous Elvis releases still held ground.

"Heroes" sold well in the UK, climbing to number three and staying on the chart for 33 weeks. In the US, it stalled at number 35, and a moderate 19-week run marked Bowie's weakest showing there since *Hunky Dory* six years

earlier, breaking his streak of four top 20 albums in a row. The album performed strongly across several countries, charting high in the Netherlands, Australia, Italy, Norway, Sweden, New Zealand, France and Austria, with more modest placements in Canada, Germany and Japan.

On release, it drew considerable praise from the music press, though not without dissent. *NME* called it Bowie's 'most moving performance in years' and counted it among the most mature and trenchant works he had achieved. *Melody Maker* described it and its predecessor as 'among the most adventurous and notably challenging records yet thrust upon the rock audience.' *ZigZag* called it 'a strange, cold, sometimes impenetrable album', but added that 'Bowie makes all these unlikely ingredients work.' *Record Mirror* struck a more ambivalent tone, calling the album 'disjointed'. It criticised the instrumentals on side two for lacking the continuity found on *Low*, and described Bowie's vocals as 'hollow' and the lyrics as 'opaque'. While finding the record 'intriguing', the review singled out the title track for praise, but dubbed the rest 'clever, but not brilliant', concluding that 'you expect no less from Bowie. In that sense, it's a disappointment, a come-down from *Low*.'

In the US, *Rolling Stone* highlighted Eno's role and argued that, unlike on *Low*, where Bowie's use of him amounted to 'auteurist exploitation', *"Heroes"* felt more like a true collaboration, a union of Bowie's dramatic instincts and Eno's unshakable sonic serenity. *Billboard* called the album an 'extension' of both 'Bowie's cosmic rock vision' and *Low*, describing it as 'a musical excursion into a realm only Bowie himself can define'. *Creem* found merit in side one but dismissed side two, concluding that *"Heroes"* 'doesn't rock'. *The Village Voice* also took issue with the instrumentals, calling them 'interesting background' but 'merely noteworthy as foreground, admirably rather than attractively ragged', especially when compared to their counterparts on *Low*. The *LA Times* criticised Bowie's fluctuating pop interests, arguing that he moved from style to style faster than he could master them, and called the album one of his 'least arresting turns'. In the *Village Voice*'s annual Pazz & Jop critics' poll, it finished 21st in the voting for 1977's top albums.

Beyond the critical reception, the album resonated with fellow artists. John Lennon is reported to have said that his ambition when making *Double Fantasy* in 1980 was to 'do something as good as *"Heroes"*.' Patti Smith's *Hit Parader* piece on *"Heroes"*, published in April 1978 under the title 'Heroes: A Communique', reads like a fever dream: part fan letter, part poetic invocation. Writing from Köln, in the shadow of RAF terrorism and urban alienation, she casts Bowie as a 'neo-somnambulist', a mythic drifter 'escaping into life'. The album, she writes, is 'a cryptic product of a high order of intelligence', 'committed to survival', with the title track capturing 'that desperate moment when one will die for love.' For Smith, *"Heroes"* was not just a record but a transmission from the ruins, a soundtrack for beauty, collapse and the longing to transcend both.

She also noted that the boys who first played her the album in Köln described Bowie's performance as 'not rock 'n' roll' but 'cabaret'. Their reaction points to the album's unmistakable theatrical streak, where restrained emotion meets stylised drama, and performance walks the line between sincerity and pose. The record thrives on this tension, while the backlit staging and measured delivery in the video of '"Heroes"' recalls 'Maybe This Time' from the film *Cabaret*. A Berlin club singer whispering 'Liebling' into an otherwise English song, or Bowie adopting an affected croon in 'The Secret Life Of Arabia', only deepens the theatrical feel. It is a finger-snap to Fassbinder or Brecht: cabaret made strange, fractured and grotesque. 'I think I'm the most unlikely contender to be in rock 'n' roll. I think I probably would have been far better suited to another time, for sort of vaudeville or cabaret or something', Bowie told *Lola Da Musica* in 1996.

Brecht's epic theatre plays were often non-linear and episodic, built on a deliberately loose structure with scenes arranged in seemingly arbitrary order. It is a method that echoes through the fragmented narratives of *Ziggy Stardust*, *Diamond Dogs*, *Outside* and *Lazarus*. Bowie's vision for the 1987 *Glass Spider Tour* also drew on the stylised, declamatory force of expressionist theatre, especially in the work of Georg Kaiser and Brecht.

Brecht had little patience for the folkloristic song culture that gained popularity after German unification in the 1870s. He saw these *Volkslieder* as relics, bound to a bygone era that had nothing to say to the workers of contemporary Munich. He preferred throwaway tunes, jazz, kitsch: music that could seduce, jar, or destabilise. In collaboration with composer Kurt Weill, these lowbrow sources were refined into musical theatre that unsettled as much as it entertained. Bowie had shown a clear fascination ever since Lindsay Kemp introduced him to Brecht in the 1960s. In Berlin, he would regularly cross into the East on a day visa to attend performances at the Berliner Ensemble, the legendary theatre company founded by Brecht himself. The Brecht-Weill opera *The Rise And Fall Of The City Of Mahagonny* had already echoed through *Ziggy Stardust*, and Bowie gave operatic treatment to their 'Alabama Song', performing it during the *Stage Tour* and recording it during a break in 1978. That same year, Bowie was considered for Fassbinder's planned adaptation of the Brecht-Weill *Threepenny Opera*, though the production was never realised. In September 1981, Bowie returned to Hansa to record five songs for the *David Bowie In Bertolt Brecht's Baal* EP. It was his final Hansa session, once again produced by Visconti using the three-microphone technique.

Back in October 1977, when Bowie embarked on an intensive European promotional campaign following the release of *"Heroes"*, he told *Melody Maker*:

> Both *Low* and *"Heroes"* have been met with confused reactions. That was to be expected, of course. But I didn't promote *Low* at all, and some

> people thought my heart wasn't in it. This time, I wanted to put everything into pushing my new album. I believe in the last two albums, you see, more than anything I have done before. I mean, I look back on a lot of my earlier work and, although there's much that I appreciate about it, there is not a great deal that I actually like. I don't think they are very likeable albums at all. There is a lot more heart and emotion in *Low* and, especially, the new album.

Bowie, who had overcome his fear of flying for the North Atlantic *The Idiot Tour* six months earlier, followed the *"Heroes"* campaign with a private trip to Aberdare National Park in Kenya, accompanied by six-year-old Zowie. The journey was partly to show him animals in their natural habitat, and also to engage with local cultures, including the Maasai and Giriama, whose musical traditions left a strong impression.

In November, he introduced Devo on stage at Max's Kansas City in New York, telling the audience he would produce the band's first album in Tokyo over the winter. They were caught off guard by the unexpected announcement, but eager to follow through. The plan never materialised: filming had already been scheduled to begin in January for *Schöner Gigolo, Armer Gigolo*, also known as *Just A Gigolo*, a lavishly financed production with Bowie in the leading role.

As 1977 drew to a close, Bowie made appearances on both *90 Minutes Live* and *Good Morning America*. His final recording of the year was Prokofiev's *Peter And The Wolf*, which he later described as a Christmas present to Zowie. His narration was taped at RCA Studios in New York, set to a pre-recorded performance by the Philadelphia Orchestra conducted by Eugene Ormandy. After Alec Guinness and Peter Ustinov had passed on the project, Ormandy had no idea who the narrator would be, and when told it was Bowie, the name meant nothing to him. But hearing the final result, he was quietly impressed. Bowie's reading brought an unexpected warmth, a gentle clarity and a lightness of touch. He didn't settle into a single narrator voice but shifted character throughout: the cat voiced with sleek insinuation, the grandfather delivered with a gruff severity, the little bird given a sudden, fluttering delicacy. Naturally, Bowie turned out to be a fitting guide for younger listeners, effortlessly suggesting that voice and identity could slip into other shapes with ease.

The promotional slogan for the LP asked: 'What happens when a world-famous maestro teams up with a pop-rock dynamo?' As it turned out: a Grammy nomination for Best Recording for Children, a number 136 spot on the US *Billboard* chart and warm critical praise for Bowie's narration. On release, *Rolling Stone* wrote that he had found 'his most charming guise since *Hunky Dory*.' *Sounds* praised the album as an ideal introduction to classical music for children, or for anyone 'who's a child of all ages', while the *Reno Gazette-Journal* found it 'surprisingly refreshing' and noted: 'For David Bowie fans, it is another successful demonstration of his openness to new directions.'

As Christmas settled over Berlin, Bowie, Coco and friends dined at a secluded restaurant in the Grunewald, the dark forest stretching along the city's western edge. A brief pre-Christmas attempt at reconciliation with Angie in Switzerland had collapsed, and Bowie was set to file for divorce in early 1978. He spent the last week of 1977 in Berlin with Zowie. It was the close of an exceptionally prolific period: two solo albums and two albums he produced for Iggy, all released that year; *The Idiot Tour*, an international promotional run, a successful foray into narration and *"Heroes"* crowned Album of the Year by both *NME* and *Melody Maker*, with *Sounds* placing it tenth. In the *NME* Readers' Poll, Bowie was voted Best Male Singer, as he had been in 1973 and 1974.

Among the accolades and creative gains, there had also been one sudden, personal loss: his longtime 'frenemy' Marc Bolan. The two had first met as teenagers, and their bond was defined by a mix of rivalry and admiration that fuelled both careers. On 7 September, they had filmed together for Bolan's TV show, where a slipping microphone stand sent Bolan to the floor. Bowie, amused, quipped: 'A wooden box for Marc to stand on, please.' Just over a week later, Bolan would be dead.

In the early hours of 16 September, Bolan and his partner Gloria Jones, mother of their two-year-old son Rolan, were returning home from a night out when Jones lost control of their Mini. The car hit a fence post, then a tree. Jones was left critically injured; Bolan died at the scene, two weeks short of his 30th birthday.

Bowie flew in from Switzerland for the funeral, shaken both by the loss and by the harassment of fans outside the service. In the years that followed, he quietly paid for Rolan's private schooling and offered further financial support. Rolan told *The Daily Mail* in 2011: 'David's generosity helped my mother and me to survive. It wasn't just the financial help, but the time and kindness.'

Stagecraft

The year opened under another cloud. In early 1978, Angie sold her story to the *Sunday Mirror*, trading on the wreckage of the marriage, and was soon after admitted to Samaritan Hospital in Vevey following what was reportedly one of several suicide attempts. Bowie, meanwhile, was in Berlin with Zowie, filming *Just A Gigolo* with English director David Hemmings.

Set in post-World War I Berlin, the film follows a Prussian officer who becomes a hired companion in a decadent, collapsing society during Hitler's rise. Promoted as 'the most expensive German post-war film', it fell far short of its obvious role model, *Cabaret*, was mercilessly panned by critics and is now largely forgotten. Alongside Bowie, the cast included Sydne Rome, Kim Novak and Marlene Dietrich in her final screen role, a prospect that helped persuade Bowie to take the part. After six months of lobbying by the producer, Dietrich was coaxed out of retirement, reportedly receiving $250,000 for two days of filming. She and Bowie never met: they spoke on the phone and sent postcards to each other, but Dietrich refused to leave Paris. Much to Bowie's disappointment, her brief scenes were shot there and later edited into the Berlin footage.

It is easy to see why Bowie was drawn to the part. With its fusion of Weimar imagery, Dietrich mythos and his own Berlin surroundings, *Just A Gigolo* folded his fascinations, fictions and lived reality into a single tableau. Scenes were shot in Schöneberg, at the Schlosshotel Gehrhus in Grunewald, where he had stayed upon arriving in Berlin in 1976, and at the Lützower Lampe in Charlottenburg, the setting of his 31st birthday party with Iggy and Eno. He could hardly have come closer to the atmosphere that had fuelled his imagination. This was Bowie in essence, willing an illusion into being until it became real.

Bowie contributed a song to the soundtrack, the quasi-Brecht-Weill piece 'Revolutionary Song', featuring his own 'lalala'-ing in a melody faintly reminiscent of 'Velvet Goldmine'. Co-written with musical director Jack Fishman and fleshed out by a mystery studio group called The Rebels, the track was released only in Japan as a single and has remained a cult curio for completists.

The film opened in Berlin in November 1978 but was swiftly pulled after poor reviews. A recut version premiered in London three months later, but reception remained scathing: *Time Out* advised readers to 'overlook it', and the *Sunday Mirror* called the film 'all show and no substance', describing Bowie as 'completely miscast'. Largely ignored by audiences, *Just A Gigolo* soon slipped into obscurity. Although Bowie had enjoyed the filming and held Hemmings in high regard, he, too, was disappointed by the incoherent cut. In *NME* in 1980, he told the interviewer: 'Listen, you were disappointed, and you weren't even in it. Imagine how we felt ... It was my 32 Elvis Presley movies rolled into one.' Seven years later, his verdict was sharper, though he was quick to put things in perspective. 'It was an *atrocious* movie; but there again, all it was was an atrocious movie, I mean it's not the end of the world or anything like that. When one starts out one's career with 'Laughing Gnome', it's very easy to just put things down to experience', he told *i-D* magazine.

After filming wrapped, Bowie once again travelled to Kenya, then flew to Dallas to attend rehearsals in a large, windowless warehouse for his most expansive tour yet. He was eager to bring his new material to the stage, though he viewed the prospect of relentless travel with growing weariness. The financial return, however, was difficult to overlook. Alongside the DAM trio, he had wanted Fripp and Eno to join the band, but both declined, reluctant to return to the demands of a full-scale tour. Instead, he brought in Sean Mayes from Fumble on keys, Simon House from Hawkwind on violin and, on Eno's recommendation, Roger Powell from Utopia on synths. Following another tip from Eno, he had lured guitarist Adrian Belew away from Frank Zappa's band. At a Berlin show, which Bowie had attended to check him out, Belew spotted him and Iggy by the monitors during one of Zappa's meandering solos and went over for a quiet word. Bowie immediately sounded him out about joining his band. Later that night, he tried to arrange a discreet meeting, only to walk into the same restaurant as Zappa and his entourage. Zappa refused to acknowledge him, spitting: 'Fuck you, Captain Tom.' Belew recalled on his blog in 2007: 'No matter what David tried, Frank kept saying, 'fuck you, Captain Tom.' So we left the restaurant. Outside, David said, 'That went down rather well, didn't it?''

Zappa ultimately relented, and after the tour, watched with ill-concealed resentment as his guitarist left for Bowie, who was about to bring *Low* and *"Heroes"* to life onstage for the first time. The two albums served as both anchor and launchpad: their sounds and aesthetics now reimagined in concert, in visual design and in live performance. Promotional posters and the official programme featured a charcoal drawing by Bowie himself, a self-aware, caricatured mutation of his *"Heroes"* cover portrait. RCA reproduced it as a limited-edition lithograph to promote the US leg of the tour, with 120 of the 250 prints signed by Bowie and handed out to contest winners at American record shops.

The *Stage Tour* opened in San Diego on 29 March 1978 with a setlist that stayed largely consistent through nearly 80 shows across North America, Europe, Australia and New Zealand before concluding at the Nippon Budokan in Japan at the end of the year. The nature of the new albums had alienated some veteran Bowie fans – in Detroit, a large banner hung from the balcony read 'Bring Back Old Bowie' – but overall his core audience embraced the expanded range of his repertoire. Bowie set the tone with a bold opener in 'Warszawa', leading into a powerful rendition of '"Heroes"', in which he soon began singing a striking new high note in the fourth verse: 'And YOU would be my queen'. Pianist Sean Mayes later wrote in *Life On Tour With David Bowie*: 'Every time it would give me a lift. When he didn't sing it, I felt cheated.'

"Heroes" was represented further by 'Beauty And The Beast', 'Sense Of Doubt' and 'Blackout', alongside selections from *Low*, mainstays 'Fame', 'The Jean Genie' and 'Rebel Rebel', and half of *Station To Station*. He debuted 'Alabama Song', bringing his own strain of Berlin cabaret and Brecht-Weill kink to a wide audience, much as The Doors had done a decade earlier. Most surprising was the return of *Ziggy Stardust* material, performed with its original punch but reframed through synth sheen and prog-tinged electric violin. 'It's a very fine line', Bowie told *The New York Times* that year, on the tension between entertainment and experiment. 'I'm not quite as much of an extremist as most of the people that I admire. I'm doing what I'm best at doing. However much I'd like to become an avant-gardist, that is not in the cards.'

Reprising the expressionist banks of white neon from the *Station To Station Tour*, now set against a stage flashing in shifting colours, a healthy, tanned and well-voiced Bowie appeared in a rotating wardrobe that fused nautical touches, bohemian flourishes and theatrical flair. Centrepieces included a snakeskin jacket, a silk Hawaiian-style shirt and a double-breasted mess coat, paired with voluminous trousers cut like Jacobean breeches but tailored in full-length drill. Each night, he chose a different mix: sailor whites, loose pastel or tie-dye shirts, and a sailor cap during the finale. The result was a stage persona at once casual and stylised, blending the seafarer's nonchalance with the panache of a travelling European nightclub crooner performing in a sultry lounge adrift in tropical light. Bowie moved between the spectral minimalism of the 'Berlin' instrumentals and the souped-up glam of his past with striking precision, commanding both without breaking stride.

Critics praised the tour's visual flair, energy and charm. *Rolling Stone* highlighted its cohesion despite the breadth of material, noting 'the most surprising aspect of his new live show is the ease with which he melds the disparate strands into a tightly woven whole.' *The Pittsburgh Press* wrote that 'he proved what he has hidden under excessive theatrics all these years: that he's one of the very best rock 'n' rollers around', while *The New York Times* hailed a Madison Square Garden concert as 'one of the highlights of the year.' *NME* lauded Bowie's magnetic presence, calling the band 'the tightest outfit he's ever worked with, and that includes The Spiders', and described the white neon strip-lighting as 'dazzling'.

With the tour in full swing, plans to capture it for release were set in motion. In spring, Visconti came on board to record what was essentially a contractual live album, compiled from shows in Philadelphia, Providence and Boston. Released in September 1978, while the tour was yet to reach its final destinations in the Southern Hemisphere, the resulting double album became a commercial success, reaching number five in the UK and later certified gold. In the US, it peaked at number 44 on the *Billboard* chart and reached the top ten in the Netherlands and New Zealand.

Despite its chart presence, *Stage* met with mixed responses. The mix prioritised clarity over atmosphere: direct instrument feeds and reduced crowd noise took precedence, with fades between tracks mimicking a studio record. The chronological running order, suggested by Visconti and approved by Bowie, further distanced it from the live experience of the actual concerts. Instrumentals raised eyebrows, sounding almost indistinguishable from their studio counterparts. Even the packaging was criticised, not least because the cover featured little more than variations of the same, rather muted photograph. Later reissues would attempt to correct the album's original shortcomings. The 1991 Rykodisc CD release kept the original running order but added 'Alabama Song' as a bonus track. A 2005 remaster restored the actual setlist sequence and added 'Be My Wife' and 'Stay'. In the 2017 *A New Career In A New Town* box set, 'The Jean Genie' and 'Suffragette City' were included, pushing the album closer to the full scope of the 1978 shows. Even so, no reissue could quite revive its reputation as one of Bowie's more contested live albums: more studio artefact than visceral live recording. Even at the time, many favoured *David Live* for its radically reworked arrangements and fervent theatrical sweat, or turned to the then-unofficial Santa Monica or Hammersmith Odeon tapings.

Still, an alternative take proves equally persuasive. Bowie's vocals are masterful throughout, at times unmatched. The band play with tight control and occasional flashes of fire, while the setlist ventures into darker corners without abandoning the hits. A stretched-out 'Breaking Glass', ending in the obsessive loop of the 'I'll never touch you' coda, is fiercely effective. Versions of 'Station To Station' and 'Fame' are simply blistering. The reggae-laced opening of 'What In The World' feels playful and inventive, and Bowie's vocal performance on '"Heroes"' stands among the finest he ever captured on tape. And this on a live album.

While the Ziggy numbers lack Mick Ronson's electrically charged bite, they remain striking, though cast in a different instrumental palette. The sped-up 'Soul Love' receives a synth treatment that skirts the edge of cheesiness but stays curiously compelling. 'Five Years' may miss the original's harrowing wails, but Bowie's phrasing, tone and delivery add another shade of despair to the song: more sorrowful resignation than manic reckoning with impending doom. The 'Ziggy Stardust' riff, reimagined in a sweep of violin and synths, works surprisingly well, and Bowie's long 'plaaaaayed ... guitar' never fails to deliver its soaring payoff. That fusion of an older song with a synthetic sonic language is emblematic of the transitional moment Bowie was stepping into: not disowning the past, but filtering it through a forward-looking lens. A stylised and emotionally modulated approach that would become the signature of the New Romantic and art-pop scenes of the early 1980s. It marked the first contours of a transformation that would, over the next few years, see Bowie shift from radical innovator to a defining figure in a new kind of pop stardom. But first, there was a triptych to be completed.

The Last Frame

Bowie had spoken of a third and final instalment ever since promoting *"Heroes"*. After a two-month break from the tour, Bowie, Visconti, Eno and the touring band regrouped in Switzerland in September to begin work on the projected close of the Bowie-Eno trilogy, then still going by working titles including *Despite Straight Lines, Look Back In Anger* and *Planned Accidents*, the latter echoed in the final album cover.

They set up in the smaller of two rooms at Mountain Studio, soon crammed with musicians, gear and competing ideas. The sessions mirrored the approach of the first sides of *Low* and *"Heroes"*: lean rhythm tracks laid down by the DAM trio, then layered with synths, guitars and effects. Lyrics were developed separately, with vocals and occasional overdubs by Belew and Powell added at The Record Plant in New York in March 1979.

'It's often struck me that there will usually be one track on any given album of mine which will be a fair indicator of the intent of the following album', Bowie told *Uncut* in 1999. In the case of *"Heroes"*, that insight may have applied to more than one track: 'Neukölln', 'Moss Garden' and 'The Secret Life Of Arabia' each point ahead, with their outward gaze, exotic textures and hints of cultural hybridity within a Western pop framework. *Lodger* would take those impulses further, expanding them into a restless panorama of travel, displacement and cultural collision, where familiar song forms were bent and stretched by the pressures of a wider world. Bowie steps away from the more abstract, ambient dimension of the instrumental sides of *Low* and *"Heroes"*, turning instead to more direct song structures, shot through with colour, angularity and surprise. The album's character emerges from that friction: a negotiation between accessibility and experiment, between the conventional and the disruptive. Its musical language extends rock's vocabulary with reggae, Middle Eastern motifs, funk and other tonalities beyond the Western canon, prefiguring the global forays of artists like Peter Gabriel and Paul Simon in the 1980s.

Beneath that surface runs a dual thematic current: one concerned with movement and migration, the other with a critique of Western civilisation and its centre-bound perspective. Bowie's projection as a lodger, neither rooted nor fully detached, is at once self-image and persona, and stands in direct literary lineage with Kerouac's spirit of endless motion, Isherwood's subtle portrait of the eternal passer-by and Dos Passos' travellers through time and society, all of them later included in Bowie's list of 100 favourite books. Chatwin's *The Songlines*, published in 1987 and also part of that selection, echoes the same state: a man who lives in transit, for whom each border crossing becomes a point of transformation. The album could have been called *Travel Along With Bowie*, as Bowie remarked on Capital Radio in 1979.

During the sessions, Bowie and Eno contrasted the traditional method of songwriting with the open, process-driven approach they had already explored on *Low* and *"Heroes"*. On Capital Radio, Bowie explained that they would sometimes set strict, almost game-like constraints for the musicians:

> The kinds of things Brian and I were doing were like: 'Look, here's 50 seconds. Play ten notes in those 50 seconds, and don't repeat the same note twice.' And then they'd all have to do that. Then we might make that into a tape loop and write something over it. It was that kind of feeling, rather than sitting down at the piano and writing something that's supposed to fulfil the artist's concept of something. There's no governor, no controller: that's the point.

Another experiment saw Eno pulling out a blackboard marked with chords and using a teacher's pointer to direct the baffled DAM trio to switch mid-groove. 'This was not, on the face of it, Brian's finest idea', Visconti recalled in *Bowie, Bolan And The Brooklyn Boy*. 'I could see the rhythm section exchanging irritable looks as if to say 'what an asshole." Other approaches proved more fruitful, and added to the off-kilter brilliance of a record that remains too often treated as the awkward dinner guest at the Berlin table.

The Cold War tension Bowie had immersed himself in since 1976 surfaces in 'Fantastic Voyage', originally titled 'Portrait Of An Artist'. Opening the album with disarming gentleness, it fuses geopolitical anxiety with a weary emotional tone, drifting between detachment and despair. The song protests a system that normalises psychological and political damage. In a world shaped by state crime and the threat of ideological violence, Bowie moves between the personal and the collective. His lyrics voice defining fears: that we may never grow old, as destruction lies in the hands of a paranoid, unstable leader.

First worked up under the name 'Burning Eyes', 'African Night Flight' began as a jam sparked by playing Dale Hawkins' 'Suzy Q' backwards. It stands as one of Bowie's most bizarre recordings, foreshadowing the fractured rhythmic hybrids and cross-cultural textures Eno would soon explore with Talking Heads and David Byrne. Eno provided what the credits called 'cricket menace': chattering pulses generated with his EMS Synthi and a drum machine. He also rigged the piano with scissors and metal objects placed between the strings, giving it a clanging, ceremonial undertone. Bowie raps at dizzying speed, set against an impressionistic pseudo-African chant. The lyrics draw on his time in Kenya, where he encountered mysterious German pilots in Mombasa bars, some reportedly ex-Luftwaffe. Their presence echoes through the song's feverish imagery, as displaced men drift across landscapes in prop planes, half dream, half menace.

After listening to 'All The Young Dudes' backwards, Bowie was taken by the odd, strangled melody that emerged. He had the band learn the reversed sequence for a piece initially titled 'The Tangled Web We Weave', which later developed into the galloping 'Move On'. A travelogue in motion, the lyric is strikingly direct yet emotionally layered, capturing a restless pull towards new horizons, laced with a quiet, unresolved ache. A veiled farewell to Berlin, perhaps.

In 'Yassassin', Bowie tentatively ululates over the skanking groove, voicing a guest worker's perspective – as discussed in the 'Neuköln' chapter – in a track that fuses Hijazkar-tinged violin, reggae rhythm and funk inflections into a curious, border-crossing hybrid.

Bowie was already into Neu! during the *Diamond Dogs* sessions, with 'Chant Of The Ever Circling Skeletal Family' echoing 'Negativland' from their 1972 debut. On 'Red Sails', he draws from Neu!'s 'Hero' and Harmonia's 'Monza (Rauf Und Runter)', a 1975 track by the trio of Cluster's Roedelius and Moebius with Neu! guitarist Rother. 'Here we took a German new music feel and put it against the idea of a contemporary English mercenary-cum-swashbuckling Errol Flynn, and put him in the China Sea', Bowie told *Melody Maker* in 1979. The title may recall the mention of 'red sails' in Eliot's *The Waste Land*, also on Bowie's list of favourite books, though he left the song's meaning deliberately vague: 'I honestly don't know what it's about.' Closing the travel side with the hooky chant from the margins, 'The hinterland, the hinterland/We're gonna sail to the hinterland', Bowie reasserts his role as musical nomad and aesthetic traveller.

Side two opens with 'D.J.', originally planned as 'I Bit You Back', a satirical swipe at celebrity, stardom and identity. In 1978, the DJ was not yet a fully fledged cultural icon, but his rise as performer and persona was unmistakable. Bowie was quick to catch on: he observes and parodies the disc jockey as both guru and void, a public figure defined entirely by appearance and surface effect. The result is an ironic take on the performative self, a world where presence is everything and substance nothing. The DJ becomes a hollow belief system, seen solely for what he plays. The lyrics lament routine, cultural exhaustion and mental depletion. Bowie's character loses his grip on reality, relationships and identity: 'I am a D.J., I am what I play'. The abbreviation doubles as caricature and clue, folding David Jones into one disintegrating persona.

Driven by Davis' rapid-fire drumming and Bowie's furious, incantatory delivery, 'Look Back In Anger', first conceived as 'Fury', presents its angelic figure as a disillusioned incarnation of death, fatigued and unresponsive in the face of human reckoning. He arrives solemnly, coughing and shaking his crumpled wings, like a jaded civil servant of fate. Yawning, leafing through a magazine, stalled in his own inertia, he is a rusted cog lodged in a brilliantly kinetic track of controlled combustion.

Bowie had wanted to capture a garage band feel for 'Boys Keep Swinging', built on the same chord sequence as 'Fantastic Voyage'. He and Eno agreed that the best way to get there was to have the musicians swap instruments, prompted by an *Oblique Strategies* card reading 'Reverse roles'. 'They all became 12-year-olds', Bowie amusingly recalled in *Musician* in 1995. Alomar took the drums, Murray made a brief and abortive stab at the piano, while Davis moved to bass, though his part was so shambolic that Visconti quietly re-recorded it himself. Inspired by Fripp's improvised blind solos on *"Heroes"*, Bowie applied a similar method with Belew. Working without hearing the songs in advance or knowing their key, Belew recorded wailing, discordant guitar parts for 'Red Sails', 'D.J.' and 'Boys Keep Swinging' in three takes apiece. Bowie and Visconti later mined the results for the most striking phrases, stitched into the final mix like a Burroughs cut-up. 'I definitely think I could have come up with different things if I'd had the time to learn the songs and really work on them', Belew told *Guitar Player* in 2023. 'I do quite like the way that they turned out, though, because it was very unusual. In a way, it started me down that road of people thinking that that was how I played. So I did.'

'The idea of 'Boys' was to write an ultra-chauvinist overkill song, and do it strictly tongue in cheek. I find it very amusing', Bowie said on WNEW-FM in 1979. The track sounds breezy, but its undercurrent is loaded. Beneath the ramshackle pop bounce lies a cold dissection of how masculinity is rewarded, promoted and weaponised. It lists the perks of being born male in the post-war West: sex, status, ownership and preferential treatment. But one line skews the perspective. With 'Other boys check you out', the gaze turns inward, tinting the parade of male privilege with a flash of ambiguity, hinting at flirtation, judgment, or both. Bowie sings of uniforms and unfurled flags, collapsing boyhood into a script of discipline, entitlement and patriotic display. It sketches a culture where male privilege bleeds cleanly into nationalism and militarism. 'The glory in that song was ironic. I do not feel that there is anything remotely glorious about being either male or female. I was merely playing on the idea of the colonisation of a gender', Bowie told *BUST* in 2000. He returned to the boy-in-uniform in 2013 with 'I'd Rather Be High', now stripped of bravado and illusion, no longer swinging but drafted, dazed and afraid.

In the promotional video for 'Boys', Bowie appears as both a swaggering, schoolboy Elvis and in drag as three parodic female figures: one resembling Bet Lynch, another styled after Marlene Dietrich and a third evoking Lauren Bacall. The performance flips male bravado through camp theatre and deliberate exaggeration. At its core, it is creative satire, complete with wig-ripping and lipstick-smearing gestures borrowed from Romy Haag's stage act, which she later criticised him for. The BBC received a wave of complaints, but the single still reached number seven on the UK charts. RCA America, sensing trouble, blocked a US release altogether.

Bowie name dropped Kierkegaard twice on his 1979 *Star Special* for BBC Radio 1, joking that he had 'read him on a wall', a fitting image for the way the lodger absorbs ideas by wandering, collecting fragments, slogans and stray thoughts. 'Repetition', working title 'Emphasis On Repetition', refers both to its nagging musical grind and to the flat, numbed pattern of life it depicts.

Cynically and cleverly placed after 'Boys Keep Swinging', it shows how the promise of a chauvinist, masculinist society curdles into disillusionment: Johnny's life becomes an endless loop of work, frustration and domestic violence, framed by the belief that his disappointments are someone else's fault. In Kierkegaard's *Repetition*, a young man abandons his engagement after confronting the impossibility of reliving love's original intensity, fearing that marriage would trap him in a hollow structure of repetition. Bowie's Johnny is caught in the same existential cycle: the repeated line 'He could have married Anne with the blue silk blouse' haunts him as the ghost of a life he never lived. For both Kierkegaard and Bowie, marriage becomes a metaphor for repetition's failure, as love reduced to routine turns promise into regret. In Bowie's version, repetition also manifests in the violence and suffocating reality that entraps the beleaguered spouse: 'Don't hit her', Bowie chillingly says, as Johnny comes home to a dinner that's been waiting, now cold. 'There's a numbness to the whole rhythm section that I try to duplicate with a deadpan vocal, as though I'm reading a report rather than witnessing the event', Bowie wrote in 2008 for the *Daily Mail*.

'Red Money' closes the Berlin era in circular fashion. Built on the backing track of Iggy's 'Sister Midnight', the opener of *The Idiot*, Bowie added backward guitar, vocal harmonies and the wry refrain 'project cancelled'. His explanation in *Melody Maker* in 1979 that the red box in the lyrics – a mysterious object that cannot be dropped, passed on, or ignored, and which also appears in his paintings – symbolises responsibility resonates with the underlying concerns of the album. Unlike *Low*'s introversion or the outward thrust of *"Heroes"*, *Lodger* confronts complicity. From global stakes in 'Fantastic Voyage' to cycles of abuse in 'Repetition', the social reflection of 'Yassassin', the mocking take on masculinity in 'Boys Keep Swinging' and the passive nihilism of 'D.J.', a thread of personal and collective accountability runs through the album. Its final line seals the message: 'Such responsibility. It's up to you and me'.

All three Berlin-era albums reflect Bowie's engagement with Eno's methods: a willingness to embrace unpredictability, chance procedures and structural looseness. On *Low*, most of the first side had already been recorded before Eno added his overdubs. On *"Heroes"*, he was present from the start and played alongside the band, but those tracks were recorded so quickly that his presence was felt more in shaping the album's sonic character: treatments, textures and tonal atmospheres. On both albums, his influence was most pronounced on the instrumental second sides, though his processed signature was central to the sound of the first.

On *Lodger*, Eno played a more prominent role throughout, including in structuring the band recordings, in what was Bowie and Eno's most evenly co-written and arguably most stylistically diverse collaboration. Yet despite its six co-writes – more than *Low* and *"Heroes"* combined – Bowie was drifting back, with increasing pull, towards narrative songwriting and the thrill of uncalculated play. He seemed to be tiring of Eno's insistent conceptual framework, and when the record was finished in New York, Eno was no longer involved. In a 1980 *NME* interview, Bowie voiced doubts about 'this endless conceptualising' on recent Eno and Fripp albums, calling some of their theories 'fascinating', but the resulting music 'unremittingly dull'.

Eno later confirmed in *Mojo* in 2007 that the creative momentum behind the trilogy had 'petered out' by the time of *Lodger*. 'The Eno experiments had waned', Alomar told *Guitar World* in 2024, while Belew had also sensed the spark was fading: 'They didn't quarrel or anything uncivilised like that, they just didn't seem to have the spark that I imagine they might have had during the *"Heroes"* album', he recalled in *Strange Fascination*. Visconti agreed: 'I could tell that the partnership had run its natural course on that album', he said in *Mojo* in 2017. 'Brian and I had set ourselves the goal of completing a trilogy of albums', Bowie reflected in *Interview* in 1995. 'We achieved that, and we parted most amicably, and then we didn't see each other for 14 years.' The pair would not work together again until 1994, when they resumed their creative thread with the pre-millennial, angst-ridden gem *Outside*.

'David Bowie explores a new quality of life as The Lodger, on RCA Records', ran the radio commercial when *Lodger* appeared in May 1979, just as the pop landscape was shifting decisively towards new wave artists, many of them shaped by *Low* and *"Heroes"*. Measured against those two landmarks, *Lodger* was quickly regarded as the weak link in the trilogy, treated by many critics and listeners as a transitional or lesser work. *Rolling Stone* called it 'a footnote to *"Heroes"*, an act of marking time', while *Melody Maker* heard 'a nice enough pop record … slightly faceless.' *Sounds* found it 'not brilliant', and *Smash Hits* called it 'a ragbag of rejects' with only 'occasional flashes of genius.' *Record Mirror* noted its stylistic range but found the lyrics uneven.

Others were more receptive: *The New York Times* called it Bowie's 'most eloquent' album in years, while *The Village Voice* praised its ambiguity. Despite divided opinion, *Lodger* charted strongly, reaching number four in the UK and staying for 17 weeks. In the US, it peaked at number 20 on *Billboard* and remained on the chart for 15 weeks.

Both Bowie and Visconti expressed dissatisfaction with the album's mix from the outset, with critics often citing its murky, flat sound. 'I think Tony and I would both agree that we didn't take enough care mixing', Bowie told *Uncut* in 1999. 'This had a lot to do with my being distracted by personal events in my life, and I think Tony lost heart a little because it never came together as easily as *Low* and *"Heroes"* had. I would still maintain, though, that there are a number of really important ideas on *Lodger*.' Visconti echoed the sentiment on his website in 2002: 'We went to New York to finish this album, and it suffered at the mixing stage because the studios simply were not as versatile or well-equipped as their European counterparts in those days!' Despite his misgivings, he told *Uncut* in 2011: 'I play it a lot, despite how bad it sounds to me', a statement he would later overturn with the 2017 remix, which revealed the album's long-obscured richness in the *A New Career In A New Town* box set.

Two years earlier, back in the producer's chair for *Blackstar*, Visconti surprised Bowie during a vocal overdub session: he had remixed several tracks from *Lodger*. 'I said, 'Can I play you something first?" Visconti recalled in *Mojo* in 2017. 'As soon as he heard the tom fills at the start of 'Fantastic Voyage', a big smile broke out on his face. Then the special effects that were never there before. The reverb on his vocal. The guitar sound. He was so happy.'

Ghost Notes Postscript

Somewhere during the early leg of the *Stage Tour*, Bowie decided Berlin was over. Before recording the core of *Lodger* in Montreux and resuming the tour in the Asia-Pacific region, he packed up his belongings at Hauptstraße 155 and left. The coming years would find him drifting between Switzerland and New York, balancing retreat and exposure, discipline and distraction. Berlin had served its purpose: it had guided him from addiction, from the frazzled distortions of fame's shadow paranoia to something quieter, steadier. 'It took two years in Berlin to really cleanse the system', he told *Uncut* in 2001. 'I'd have days where things were moving in the room – and this was when I was totally straight!' He called Berlin his 'clinic', a place that brought him back into focus in body, spirit and sound. 'I became a person again', he recalled in a 1978 interview with *Rolling Stone*.

In his final months in the city, however, he had sensed a shift in atmosphere. By 1978, West Berlin carried a darker, more volatile mood than it had just a few years earlier, shaped by forces set in motion mid-decade that were now breaking to the surface. Around Bahnhof Zoo, the heroin scene had become a bleak feature of everyday life. Migrants in districts such as Kreuzberg, Schöneberg and Neukölln faced growing hostility, while neo-Nazi groups were finding resonance among disaffected youth. Bowie told *Arena* in 1993:

> Just before I left, the coffee bar below my apartment was smashed up by Nazis and the people were pulled out and beaten up. I went down there, and they were quite distressed. I think I gave them something for their window. And I thought – this is not a place for Joe to be growing up. This could get worse.

He decided that the peace and seclusion of Clos des Mésanges in Blonay would offer a better environment for his son to find stability. 'I want him to be a real person', Bowie told the *Daily Express* in 1979. 'Thank God he doesn't associate me with the awesome thing he sees on stage. He thinks of that as just the way Daddy makes his money. He doesn't take much interest in what I do. To him, I'm Dad – the man in the next bedroom who has breakfast with him every morning. For me, that's being real people.' When Bowie and Angie legally divorced in February 1980, Bowie was granted official custody of eight-year-old Zowie. He visited his mother on school holidays until ending contact with her at age 13. By then, he had already renamed himself Joey, later shortened to Joe. The following year, he enrolled in the Scottish co-educational boarding school Gordonstoun.

Part of Bowie's decision to stay in Switzerland was also financial: had he returned to the UK and declared his earnings there, he would have fallen into the highest income tax bracket of 83%, and on certain types of income this could have risen to as much as 98%. From 1982 to 1993, his main home was the Château de Signal, a secluded 14-room residence on the wooded slopes of Sauvabelin above Lausanne. By 1993, however, he and Iman were spending most of their time in New York, where they eventually settled permanently. The Swiss estate felt too remote for Iman, so Bowie put the castle up for sale in 1997 and sold it in 2000.

In the wake of Bowie's departure from Berlin, the city's music scene splintered outward. Squats, back rooms and repurposed spaces became incubators for noise, industrial experiments and sonic extremism. Many underground bands were part of the Geniale Dilettanten movement, a German counterpart to the UK's post-punk DIY scene that prioritised creativity and experimentation over technical skill. Most emblematic were Einstürzende Neubauten, formed in 1980, who rejected conventional instrumentation in favour of scrap metal, drills and building-site detritus, channelling the city's physical decay into explosive live performances. Around them coalesced a loose constellation of punk, new wave and minimalist acts drawn to West Berlin's vacuum of restraint. What defined the era was a shared appetite for confrontation – with form, with politics, with tradition – rather than any single, unified sound, and a spirit infused by Dadaism, German Romanticism and the decadent energy of Weimar-era culture, the very undercurrent that had drawn Bowie to Berlin in the first place.

'It's because of David that Berlin is now a great open city for rock and music', Visconti said in his 2011 Red Bull Music Academy lecture. The combination of Bowie's presence in a walled-in city of Cold War shadows, the birth of *Lust For Life* and *"Heroes"*, and the atmosphere surrounding Hansa Studios would continue to inspire and attract artists for decades. Depeche Mode, Nina Hagen, Nick Cave, Marillion, David Byrne, Supergrass, The Hives, Snow Patrol, R.E.M. and many others recorded songs and albums at Hansa in the wake of Bowie's Berlin legacy. Most famously, *Achtung Baby* was begun at Hansa in 1990, produced by Daniel Lanois with Eno. Images of the studio and other Berlin landmarks appear prominently in the sleeve art for what became U2's own reinvention album, as well as in Anton Corbijn's video for 'One'. Reflecting on his influence, Bowie told *Der Tagesspiegel* in 2002:

> Many younger artists who like my work from that time tell me they want to go to Berlin, too, to feel what I felt. Then I always tell them: that's over. You can never repeat the past. You might experience something truly great. But it will never be the way I felt it. I remember Bono, for example, he wanted to experience the same thing I did. But he had a very disappointing time in Berlin. He didn't like it at all.

Over time, Bowie's Berlin years were increasingly romanticised as a decadent, Weimar-tinged interlude of nightclubs and cabaret-lit mystique. But not everyone bought into that narrative. In a 2024 interview with *Politiken*, Neubauten frontman Blixa Bargeld offered a dryly deflating perspective: 'I don't want to talk about that – again. It's all so exaggerated; it's a giant myth. Yes, David Bowie came to West Berlin. But why? Because he wanted to go to a place where absolutely nothing happened. And he found that.' When the conversation turned to Bowie and Iggy's supposed detox period, Bargeld was equally sceptical: 'One of their sound engineers was the brother of my cocaine dealer! That's how I know they sniffed quite a bit through their noses here in the city. But I also know that a lot of it was crushed aspirin tablets because that's what he did.' In the end, though, he conceded the inevitable: 'But okay, some of the mythology is also true. They left their mark on Berlin.'

That chapter in Bowie's life would remain a cherished memory. 'It was the best thing that could have happened to me', he told *NME* in 1980, adding:

> I'd come out of the American thing with smashed ideals, inasmuch as I'd found that the ideals I did have weren't worth a shit anyway, that I was too willing to jump from point of view to point of view without taking into account the consequences of anything I was doing, just breaking out of the American cocoon. And so yes, Berlin was definitely the best place I could have gone.

Decades later, reflection gave way to feeling. What remained was not analysis but the memory of shared, quiet joy. 'I had not intended to leave Berlin, I just drifted away', he told *Uncut* in 1999. 'Maybe I was getting better. It was an irreplaceable, unmissable experience and probably the happiest time in my life up until that point. Coco, Jim and I had so many great times … I just can't express the feeling of freedom I felt there.'

In 2016, Iggy revisited their nights out at the Lützower Lampe in 'German Days', from his album *Post Pop Depression*. Three years earlier, on 8 January 2013, after almost a decade of silence, Bowie resurfaced without warning. 'Where Are We Now?' arrived like a hushed postcard from the past. The German press answered with a sudden fanfare: 'David Bowie Is Back, and Singing About Berlin', wrote *Der Tagesspiegel*; 'David Bowie Pays Homage to Berlin', ran the *Bild* headline; 'David Bowie Is Among Us Again', said *Berliner Zeitung*.

In his cryptic 2013 'workflow diagram' for *The Rumpus*, Bowie assigned three words to the song: 'Mauer', 'Interface' and 'Flitting'. Built on piano chords soaked in loss, 'Where Are We Now?' drifts through Berlin like a slow hallucination, returning to a city that no longer exists. Potsdamer Platz, once a dead zone cleaved by the Wall, is now casually traversed by train. Past encounters, lost selves and a city's buried breaks hover at the edges. A man lost in time. This quiet haunting becomes a private ritual, a mourning of what remains half-remembered and unrecoverable. Historical gravity interrupts the personal spell, with East Berliners crossing the Bösebrücke the night the Wall fell, fingers crossed, just in case. Hope is hedged with anxiety. 'Where are we now?' he muses, as if the coordinates of time, place and self have dissolved.

Fragmented images and stray impressions float through the song like smoke, borne on a frail voice uncertain whether to sing or to speak. It is both love letter and lament: a private séance in song, an act of psychic exhumation. The closing litany lingers on elemental forces – sun, rain, fire – before narrowing to a fragile connection, resting on what may be the only truth that remains: you and me. As in '"Heroes"', there is no triumph here, only a trembling hope.

The video, directed by Tony Oursler, mirrors the song's ghostly tone. Bowie's face, weathered and sombrely still, is projected onto a dummy beside Jacqueline Humphries, Oursler's wife, whose presence quietly echoes Coco, his loyal friend and PA. They sit motionless on a pommel horse in a cluttered studio, surrounded by the flotsam of memory and creative debris. Behind them, flickering images of Berlin dissolve in and out: streets, landmarks, traces of a city that had once mirrored his own fracture. At one point, a blurred image appears: Hauptstraße 155, where Bowie had once tried to vanish, and found the shape of a future self. The resonance of that era continues: from BBC documentaries and gallery retrospectives to the 2025 *Back To Berlin Tour* with Alomar, Murray and Armstrong honouring both Bowie and Dennis Davis.

With the European decadent cool of *The Idiot* – shaped by 'the idea of Berlin', as Iggy told the BBC in 2009 – and the Hansa-infused momentum of *Lust For Life*, one could view Bowie's Berlin-era output as a pentaptych: five albums orbiting a shared creative centre, yet each with its own gravitational pull. But even the so-called Berlin trilogy is a misnomer on both fronts. *Low* was started in France and finished in Berlin, *"Heroes"* began in Berlin but was completed in Switzerland and *Lodger* was recorded between Montreux and New York. Convenient as the label may be for journalists and marketers, these three albums resist any linear narrative or causal chain. Rather than unfolding like a story, *Low*, *"Heroes"* and *Lodger* sit side by side like panels in visual art: three distinct yet interconnected works, where meaning emerges through juxtaposition, variation and internal echo. A triptych, rather than a trilogy.

Each album stands on its own terms, but together they form a composite field of mood, method and displacement. *Low* is the orange-hazed recovery of Thomas Jerome Newton, a man learning to breathe again through the valves of a machine. *Lodger* is the itinerant art-school eccentric, toting his sketchbook across continents, all drainpipe trousers and post-punk prep, collecting rhythms, textures and ideas like border stamps. *"Heroes"*, the centrepiece, plays like a monochrome art film set in a scarred city, its score shifting between near-ambient restraint and sudden bursts of distorted grandeur, with Bowie staging exile as expressionist theatre in the shadow of the watchtowers.

'It's much like walking through a busy street', Bowie said of *"Heroes"* to *Newsday* in 1977. 'Flatting in on fragmented images. You can't articulate what that street was about. Musically, it's a juxtaposition of arbitrary as well as planned statements.' At a 1977 press conference in Amsterdam, he said: 'It is such a great variety of musical information on the album, because the process was rarely the same for any two tracks.' That fragmentation is precisely what gives the album its tensile force: *"Heroes"* spans incantatory minimalism, gnarled art rock, elliptical pieces and quasi-instrumental tableaux. '*"Heroes"* was just a better *Low*', Visconti told *Uncut* in 1999, and in 2017 he summarised in *A New Career In A New Town*: 'It was more than an album. It was an adventure.'

Nearly 50 years on, *"Heroes"* still resists closure. Its tensions between discipline and instinct, technology and emotion, continue to inform how artists think about sound, structure and atmosphere. Rather than standing as a fixed artefact, it remains a living framework, open to re-reading, re-hearing and reimagining across music, film and art. Each return reveals new relations within it, and with them new possibilities of meaning. That is why *"Heroes"* endures: not as a relic, but as a record that leaves its mark on the cultural imagination and remains a point against which adventurous music measures itself.

In 1980, Bowie reflected in *NME* on a shift he traced back to *Low*, *"Heroes"* and *Lodger*: 'I think those three albums helped me to appreciate that my make-up is generally much more of a microcosm of what society is than me standing back and saying, 'This is what society is about." The triptych absorbs meaning into itself, drawing the listener into its shifting moods and fractured forms. It embodies instability, doubleness and the self as a site of interference. 'I've always just wanted to do interesting things. The sequence of *Low*, *"Heroes"* and *Lodger* was really important for me. I guess the sales stunk on those, but it was important for me to get that work done, and no doubt I'll return', Bowie said in *Musician* in 1987. At a press conference in Toronto that same year, he called them 'the most satisfying albums' he'd ever worked on. Three years later, he told the *LA Times*: 'Those albums didn't sell as well as *Young Americans*, but they were what I wanted to do, and I think they still hold up. They are not everybody's favourite of the albums I've done, but they might be my favourites.'

The triptych remained a source of ongoing personal and artistic significance. In 1995, Bowie said on MTV: 'The music from that late 1970s period, for me, definitely is a landmark in what I've done. For me, there's something that I always, either embarrassingly or exuberantly, measure my new work by.' It was a resonance that would only deepen over time. Around the turn of the millennium, Bowie told *Uncut* with quiet, unwavering conviction:

> For whatever reason, for whatever confluence of circumstances, Tony, Brian and I created a powerful, anguished, sometimes euphoric language of sounds. In some ways, sadly, they really captured, unlike anything else in that time, a sense of yearning for a future that we all knew would never come to pass. It is some of the best work that the three of us have ever done. Nothing else sounded like those albums. Nothing else came close. If I never made another album, it really wouldn't matter now; my complete being is within those three. They are my DNA.

Album Credits

"Heroes" – David Bowie
Credits as printed on the original back cover of RCA PL 12522, 1977.
Durations not included in the original print.

Side A
'Beauty And The Beast' (Bowie) 3:32
'Joe The Lion' (Bowie) 3:05
'"Heroes"' (Lyrics by Bowie/Music by Bowie-Eno) 6:07
'Sons Of The Silent Age' (Bowie) 3:15
'Blackout' (Bowie) 3:50

Side B
'V-2 Schneider' (Bowie) 3:10
'Sense Of Doubt' (Bowie) 3:57
'Moss Garden' (Bowie-Eno) 5:03
'Neukölln' (Bowie-Eno) 4:34
'The Secret Life Of Arabia' (Lyrics by Bowie/Music by Bowie-Eno-Alomar) 3:46

Personnel
David Bowie: vocals, keyboards, guitar, saxophone, koto
Carlos Alomar: rhythm guitar
Dennis Davis: percussion
George Murray: electric bass
Brian Eno: synthesisers, keyboards, guitar treatments
Robert Fripp: lead guitar

David Bowie, Tony Visconti, Antonia Maass: backing vocals
Recorded at Hansa by the Wall, Berlin
Engineers: Tony Visconti, Colin Thurston
Assistant engineers: Dave Richards, Eugene Chaplin
Mixed at Mountain Studios, Montreux
Cover photography: Sukita
Produced by David Bowie and Tony Visconti

Bonus Tracks (Rykodisc CD reissue, 1991)
'Abdulmajid' (Bowie-Eno) 3:40
'Joe The Lion' (1991 Remix) (Bowie) 3:08

Selected Bibliography

Armstrong, K., *Absolute Beginner: Memoirs Of The World's Best Least-Known Guitarist* (Jawbone Press, 2023)
Broackes, V. & Marsh, G., *David Bowie Is* (V&A Publishing, 2013)
Buckley, D., *Strange Fascination: David Bowie – The Definitive Story* (Virgin Books, 1999)
Buckley, D., *The Complete Guide To The Music Of David Bowie* (Omnibus Press, 1996)
Charlesworth, C., *David Bowie: Profile* (Proteus Books, 1981)
Clerc, B., *David Bowie: All The Songs* (Running Press Adult, 2022)
Egan, S., *Bowie On Bowie: Interviews And Encounters With David Bowie* (Chicago Review Press, 2017)
Eno, B., *A Year With Swollen Appendices* (Faber and Faber, 1996)
Hagler, T., *We Could Be: Bowie And His Heroes* (Octopus Publishing Group, 2021)
Jones, D., *David Bowie: A Life* (Windmill Books, 2017)
Jones, D., *David Bowie: The Oral History* (Three Rivers Press, 2017)
Kardos, L., *Blackstar Theory: The Last Works Of David Bowie* (Bloomsbury Academic, 2022)
MacLean, R., *Berlin: Imagine A City* (Weidenfeld & Nicolson, 2014)
Mayes, S., *Life On Tour With Bowie: A Genius Remembered* (ReadHowYouWant, 2016)
Miles, B., *Bowie In His Own Words* (Omnibus Press, 1980)
O'Connell, J., *Bowie's Books: The Hundred Literary Heroes Who Changed His Life* (Bloomsbury Publishing, 2021)
O'Leary, C., *Ashes To Ashes: The Songs Of David Bowie 1976–2016* (Repeater Books, 2019)
Paytress, M., *Bowie Style* (Omnibus Press, 2000)
Pegg, N., *The Complete David Bowie* (Titan Books, 2016)
Richie, A., *Faust's Metropolis: A History Of Berlin* (HarperCollins Publishers Ltd, 1999)
Rodgers, N., *Le Freak: An Upside Down Story Of Family, Disco, And Destiny* (Spiegel & Grau, 2011)
Rüther, T., *Heroes: David Bowie And Berlin* (Reaktion Books, 2014)
Sandford, C., *Bowie: Loving The Alien* (Warner Books, 1997)
Seabrook, T. J., *Bowie In Berlin: A New Career In A New Town* (Jawbone Press, 2008)
Slapper, C., *Bowie's Piano Man: The Life Of Mike Garson* (Backbeat Books, 2018)
Soligny, J., *David Bowie Rainbowman 1967–1980* (Monoray, 2023)
Thompson, D., *David Bowie: Moonage Daydream* (Plexus Publishing UK, 1989)
Thompson, D., *Hallo Spaceboy: The Rebirth Of David Bowie* (ECW Press, 2006)

Thomson, E. & Gutman, D., *The Bowie Companion* (Grand Central Publishing, 1996)
Tremlett, G., *David Bowie: Living On The Brink* (Carroll & Graf, 1997)
Trynka, P., *David Bowie: Starman* (Little, Brown, 2011)
Visconti, T., *The Autobiography: Bowie, Bolan And The Brooklyn Boy* (HarperCollins, 2007)
Welch, C., *We Could Be Heroes: The Stories Behind Every David Bowie Song 1970–1980* (Perseus Books Group, 1999)
Wilcken, H., *Low* (Bloomsbury Academic, 2005)

In addition to the cited sources – including books, articles, interviews, websites, videos and podcasts – brief excerpts from song lyrics are quoted for the purposes of commentary, analysis and discussion, in accordance with the fair dealing provisions of UK copyright law. All sources have been cited with care and clarity.

Note: A key *Uncut* article by Rob Hughes and Stephen Dalton, used in this book as the source for several quotations by Bowie and Visconti, was published in April 2001. It appears to be a composite of interviews conducted across different sessions, with much of its Q&A content dated 1999 on both the official Bowie site and Bowiewonderworld. This book therefore uses 1999 throughout for quotations traceable to that earlier material, citing 2001 only for passages that appear solely in the published *Uncut* feature. The recollections and perspectives shared by Bowie and Visconti are best understood as rooted in the period around the turn of the millennium. The interview material compiled by Dalton and Hughes remains an essential reference.

Would you like to write for Sonicbond Publishing?

We are mainly a music publisher, but we also occasionally publish in other genres including film and television. At Sonicbond Publishing we are always on the look-out for authors, particularly for our two main series, On Track and Decades.

Mixing fact with in depth analysis, the On Track series examines the entire recorded work of a particular musical artist or group. All genres are considered from easy listening and jazz to 60s soul to 90s pop, via rock and metal.

The Decades series singles out a particular decade in an artist or group's history and focuses on that decade in more detail than may be allowed in the On Track series.

While professional writing experience would, of course, be an advantage, the most important qualification is to have real enthusiasm and knowledge of your subject. First-time authors are welcomed, but the ability to write well in English is essential.

Sonicbond Publishing has distribution throughout Europe and North America, and all our books are also published in E-book form. Authors will be paid a royalty based on sales of their book. Further details about our books are available from www.sonicbondpublishing.com. To contact us, complete the contact form there or email info@sonicbondpublishing.co.uk